Praise for *Why Meditate?*

"In this marvelous book, Matthieu Ricard articulates the Dharma in the very same way he embodies it in his life; that is, with profound clarity, goodwill, and humility. These qualities come through on every page and make the experience of reading and practicing with this elegant and deceptively simple primer on meditation tantamount to entering into and familiarizing oneself in an ever-deepening way with the landscape of one's own truest self."

— **Jon Kabat-Zinn**, author of *Wherever You Go, There You Are* and *Coming to Our Senses*

*"This is the book on meditation that I've been waiting for. Reading it has helped me hone my personal practice, and finally I have come across the perfect book to recommend to all those interested in meditation—newcomers and experts. **Why Meditate?** is clear, accessible, deep, and practical."*

— **Tal Ben-Shahar**, author of *Happier*

"An excellent introduction to a practice that has calmed the mind for thousands of years. Profound concepts and essential instructions are explained with the utmost clarity. I highly recommend it!"

— **Judith S. Beck, Ph.D.**, director of Beck Institute for Cognitive Therapy and Research, clinical associate professor of psychology in psychiatry, University of Pennsylvania, past president, Academy of Cognitive Therapy

WHY MEDITATE?

ALSO BY MATTHIEU RICARD

Books

HAPPINESS: *A Guide to Developing*
Life's Most Important Skill

THE MONK AND THE PHILOSOPHER: *A Father and Son*
Discuss the Meaning of Life (with Jean-François Revel)

THE QUANTUM AND THE LOTUS: *A Journey to the*
Frontiers Where Science and Buddhism Meet
(with Trinh Xuan Thuan)

Text and Photographs

BHUTAN: *The Land of Serenity*

BUDDHIST HIMALAYAS
(with Olivier and Danielle Föllmi)

JOURNEY TO ENLIGHTENMENT: *The Life and World*
of Khyentse Rinpoche, Spiritual Teacher from Tibet

MONK DANCERS OF TIBET

MOTIONLESS JOURNEY:
From a Hermitage in the Himalayas

TIBET: *An Inner Journey*

Translations

THE LIFE OF SHABKAR:
The Autobiography of a Tibetan Yogin

WHY MEDITATE?

Matthieu Ricard

Translated by Sherab Chödzin Kohn

HAY HOUSE, INC.
Carlsbad, California • New York City
London • Sydney • Johannesburg
Vancouver • Hong Kong • New Delhi

Published and distributed in the United States by: Hay House, Inc.: www.hayhouse.com • **Published and distributed in Australia by:** Hay House Australia Pty. Ltd.: www.hayhouse.com.au • **Published and distributed in the United Kingdom by:** Hay House UK, Ltd.: www.hayhouse.co.uk • **Published and distributed in the Republic of South Africa by:** Hay House SA (Pty), Ltd.: www.hayhouse.co.za • **Distributed in Canada by:** Raincoast Books: www.raincoast.com • **Published in India by:** Hay House Publishers India: www.hayhouse.co.in

Design: Tricia Breidenthal • *Illustration:* Padmakara Archives

First published in France in 2008 by NiL Éditions, Paris © Matthieu Ricard, 2008

Library of Congress Cataloging-in-Publication Data

Ricard, Matthieu.
[Art de la méditation. English]
Why meditate? / Matthieu Ricard ; translated by Sherab Chodzin Kohn.
  p. cm.
Includes bibliographical references.
ISBN 978-1-4019-2663-2 (tradepaper : alk. paper) 1. Meditation--Buddhism. 2. Buddhism--Doctrines. I. Chödzin, Sherab. II. Title.
BQ5614.R5313 2010
294.3'4435--dc22

2010006721

Tradepaper ISBN: 978-1-4019-2663-2

15 14 13 12 11 10 9 8
1st edition, September 2010

Printed in the United States of America

CONTENTS

BONUS CONTENT

Thank you for purchasing *Why Meditate?* by Matthieu Ricard. This product includes a free download! To access this bonus content, please visit www.hayhouse.com/download and enter the Product ID and Download Code as they appear below.

Product ID: 5002
Download Code: ebook
For further assistance, please contact
Hay House Customer Care by phone:
US (800) 654-5126 or INTL CC+(760) 431-7695
or visit www.hayhouse.com/contact.php.
Thank you again for your Hay House purchase. Enjoy!
Hay House, Inc. • P.O. Box 5100
Carlsbad, CA 92018 • (800) 654-5126

Caution: This audio program features meditation/visualization exercises that render it inappropriate for use while driving or operating heavy machinery.

Publisher's note: Hay House products are intended to be powerful, inspirational, and life-changing tools for personal growth and healing. They are not intended as a substitute for medical care. Please use this audio program under the supervision of your care provider. Neither the author nor Hay House, Inc., assumes any responsibility for your improper use of this product.

PREFACE

Why this little book on meditation? For 40 years I have had the good fortune to study with authentic spiritual masters who inspired me and illuminated my path in life. Their precious instructions have guided my actions. I am not a teacher—I remain more than ever a student—but in the course of my travels around the world, I have frequently met people who have shared with me their wish to learn to meditate. I have tried to the best of my ability to direct them to qualified teachers, but this has not always been possible. So it is for all those people who have a sincere desire to meditate that I have collected these instructions, drawn from authentic Buddhist sources, into book form.

The real significance of meditation is inner transformation through training the mind, which is a really inspiring adventure. The exercises you will find here are taken from a tradition that is more than 2,000 years old. It is best to explore them gradually, but you may also practice them independently of each other, whether you devote only 30 minutes a day to meditation or practice more intensively in the undisturbed environment of a retreat.

As for my personal history, I had the tremendous good fortune of meeting my spiritual master, Kangyur Rinpoche, in 1967 near Darjeeling in India. I owe him whatever goodness there is in my life. After his death in 1975, I spent several years in retreat in a small wooden hut built on stilts in the forest above his monastery. For a period of 12 years, starting in 1979, I had the privilege of living in the presence of the great master Dilgo Khyentse Rinpoche and receiving his teachings. Since 1991, when he departed this world, I have often stayed in retreat in a small mountain hermitage in Nepal, a few hours away from Kathmandu, in a contemplative center founded by the Shechen Monastery, where I usually reside. These periods of retreat have without a doubt been among the most fertile times of my life.

Over the course of the last ten years, I have also participated in several scientific research programs intended to document the long-term effects of meditation practice on the brain and on behavior. This research has shown that it is possible to make significant progress in developing qualities such as attention, emotional balance, altruism, and inner peace. Other studies have also demonstrated the benefits of meditating for 20 minutes a day for a period of six to eight weeks. These benefits include a decrease in anxiety, in vulnerability to pain, and in the tendency toward depression and anger, as well as strengthening the power of attention, boosting the immune system, and increasing one's general well-being. Thus, no matter what point of view you approach it from—whether that of personal transformation, the development of altruistic love, or physical health—meditation emerges as a factor essential for leading a balanced life, rich in meaning.

It is a pity to underestimate the capacity we have to transform our minds. Each of us possesses the potential needed to free ourselves from the mental states that perpetuate our own suffering and that of others—the potential to find inner peace for ourselves and contribute to the happiness of all beings.

Part I

WHY MEDITATE?

A Lucid
Assessment

Take an honest look at yourself. Where are you in your life? What have your priorities been up till now and what do you intend doing with the time you have left?

We are a mixture of light and shadow, of good qualities and defects. Are we really the best we can be? Must we remain as we are now? If not, what can we do to improve ourselves? These are questions worth asking, particularly if we have come to the conclusion that change is both desirable and possible.

In our modern world, we are consumed from morning till night with endless activity. We do not have much time or energy left over to consider the basic causes of our happiness or suffering. We imagine, more or less consciously, that if we undertake more activities we will have more intense experiences and therefore our sense of dissatisfaction will fade away. But the truth is that many of us continue to feel let down and frustrated by our contemporary lifestyle.

The aim of meditation is to transform the mind. It does not have to be associated with any particular religion. Every one of us has a mind and every one of us can work on it.

Is Change Desirable?

Very few people would say that there is nothing worth improving about the way they live and experience the world. However, some people regard their own particular weaknesses and conflicting emotions as something rich that contributes to the fullness of their lives. They believe this particular alchemy in their character is what makes them unique and think they should learn to accept themselves the way they are. They do not realize that this attitude can lead to a life of chronic discontent. Nor do they realize that they could help themselves with just a little reflection and effort.

Imagine that someone suggested you spend an entire day tormented by jealousy. Would you want to do that? I doubt it. If, on the other hand, someone suggested you spend that same day with your heart filled with love for all beings, you would probably be quite willing to do so. I'm sure you would find that infinitely preferable to a whole day of jealousy.

As things stand now, no matter what our preferences might be, our mind is often filled with troubles. We spend a great deal of time consumed by painful thoughts, plagued by anxiety or anger, licking the wounds we receive from other people's harsh words. When we experience these kinds of difficult moments, we wish we could manage our emotions; we wish we could master our mind to the point where we could be free of these disturbing emotions. It would be such a relief. However, since we don't know how to achieve this kind of control, we take the point of view that, after all, this way of living is "normal" or "natural," and that it is "human nature." Everything that is found in nature is "natural," but that does not necessarily make everything desirable. Illness, for example, comes to everybody, but does this prevent us from consulting a doctor?

We don't want to suffer. Nobody wakes up in the morning and thinks, "Oh, if I could only suffer all day today and, if possible, every day for the rest of my life!" Whatever we are occupied with—an important task, routine work, walking in the woods, pursuing a relationship, drinking a cup of tea—we always hope we will get some benefit or satisfaction out of it, either for ourselves or others. If we thought nothing would come of our activities but suffering, we wouldn't do anything at all and we would fall into despair.

Sometimes we do have moments of inner peace, of altruistic love, of deep-felt confidence; but for the most part, these are only fleeting experiences that quickly give way to other, less pleasant ones. What if we could train the mind to cultivate these wholesome moments? No doubt it would radically change our lives for the better. Wouldn't it be wonderful to become better human beings and lead lives in which we experience inner fulfillment, while also relieving the suffering of others and contributing to their well-being?

Some people think life would be dull without inner conflict, but we are all familiar with the suffering that accompanies anger, greed, or jealousy, and we all appreciate the good feelings that go along with kindness, contentment, and the pleasure of seeing other people happy. The sense of harmony that is connected with loving others has an inherent goodness in it that speaks for itself. The same is true of generosity, patience, emotional balance, and many other positive traits. If we could learn to cultivate altruistic love and inner calm, and if at the same time the self-centered approach of the ego and the frustration that arises from it could be reduced, then our lives certainly would not lose any of their richness—quite the opposite.

Is Change Possible?

So the real question is not whether change is desirable; it is whether it is possible to change. Some people might think they can't change because their afflictive emotions are so intimately associated with their minds that it is impossible to get rid of them without destroying a part of themselves.

It is true that in general a person's character doesn't change very much over the course of life. If we could study the same group of people every few years, we would rarely find that the angry people had become patient, that the disturbed people had found inner peace, or that the pretentious people had learned humility. But as rare as such changes might be, some people do change, which shows that change is possible. The point is that our negative character traits tend to persist if we do nothing at all to change the status quo. No change occurs if we just let our habitual tendencies and automatic patterns of thought perpetuate and even reinforce themselves, thought after thought, day after day, year after year. But those tendencies and patterns can be challenged.

Aggression, greed, jealousy, and the other mental poisons are unquestionably part of us, but are they an intrinsic, inalienable part? Not necessarily. For example, a glass of water might contain cyanide that could kill us on the spot. But the same water could instead be mixed with healing medicine. In either case, H_2O, the chemical formula of the water itself, remains unchanged; in itself, it was never either poisonous or medicinal. The different states of the water are temporary and dependent on changing circumstances. In a similar way, our emotions, moods, and bad character traits are just temporary and circumstantial elements of our nature.

A FUNDAMENTAL ASPECT OF CONSCIOUSNESS

This temporary and circumstantial quality becomes clear to us when we realize that the primary quality of consciousness is simply *knowing*. Like the water in the example above, knowing or awareness is neither good nor bad in itself. If we look behind the turbulent stream of transient thoughts and emotions that pass through our minds day and night, this fundamental aspect of consciousness is always there. Awareness makes it possible for us to perceive phenomena of every kind. Buddhism describes this basic cognitive quality of the mind as luminous because it illuminates both the external world through perceptions and the inner world of sensation, emotion, reasoning, memory, hope, and fear.

Although this cognitive faculty underlies every mental event, it is not itself *affected* by any of these events. A ray of light may shine on a face disfigured by hatred or on a smiling face; it may shine on a jewel or on a garbage heap; but the light itself is neither mean nor loving, neither dirty nor clean. Understanding that the essential nature of consciousness is neutral shows us that it is possible to change our mental universe. We can transform the content of our thoughts and experiences. The neutral and luminous background of our consciousness provides us with the space we need to observe mental events rather than being at their mercy. We then also have the space we need to create the conditions necessary to transform these mental events.

JUST WISHING IS NOT ENOUGH

We have no choice about what we already are, but we can wish to change ourselves. Such an aspiration gives the mind a sense of direction. But just wishing is not enough. We have to find a way of putting that wish into action.

We don't find anything strange about spending years learning to walk, read and write, or acquire professional skills. We spend hours doing physical exercises in order to get our bodies into shape. Sometimes we expend tremendous physical energy pedaling a stationary bike that goes nowhere. To sustain such tasks requires a minimum of interest or enthusiasm. This interest comes from believing that these efforts are going to benefit us in the long run.

Working with the mind follows the same logic. How could it be subject to change without the least effort, just from wishing alone? That makes no more sense than expecting to learn to play a Mozart sonata by just occasionally doodling around on the piano.

We expend a lot of effort to improve the external conditions of our lives, but in the end it is always the mind that creates our experience of the world and translates this experience into either well-being or suffering. If we transform our way of perceiving things, we transform the quality of our lives. It is this kind of transformation that is brought about by the form of mind-training known as meditation.

WHAT IS MEDITATION?

Meditation is a practice that makes it possible to cultivate and develop certain basic positive human qualities in the same way as other forms of training make it possible to play a musical instrument or acquire any other skill.

Among several Asian words that translate as "meditation" in English are *bhavana* from Sanskrit, which means "to cultivate," and its Tibetan equivalent, *gom*, meaning "to become familiar with." Meditation helps us to familiarize ourselves with a clear and accurate way of seeing things and to cultivate wholesome qualities that remain dormant within us unless we make an effort to draw them out.

So let us begin by asking ourselves, "What do I really want out of life? Am I content to just keep improvising from day to day? Am I going to ignore the vague sense of discontent that I always feel deep down when, at the same time, I am longing for well-being and fulfillment?"

We have become accustomed to thinking that our shortcomings are inevitable and that we have to put up with the setbacks they have brought us throughout our lives. We take the dysfunctional aspects of ourselves for granted, not realizing that it is possible to break out of the vicious cycle of exhausting behavior patterns.

From a Buddhist point of view, every being has the potential for enlightenment just as surely, say the traditional texts, as every sesame seed contains oil. Despite this, to use another traditional comparison, we wander about in confusion like a beggar who is simultaneously both rich and poor because he does not know that he has a treasure buried under the floor of his hut. The goal of the Buddhist path is to come into possession of this overlooked wealth of ours, which can imbue our lives with the most profound meaning.

TRANSFORM YOURSELF TO TRANSFORM THE WORLD

Developing our own positive inner qualities is the best way to help others. At the beginning, our personal experience is our only reference point. Our personal, self-centered experience, which tells us that we don't want to suffer, can become the basis for a much larger point of view that includes all beings. We are all dependent on each other and we all aspire to happiness. It would be absurd (if not impossible) to feel happy while countless other beings all around us are miserable. Seeking happiness for oneself alone is doomed to failure, since self-centeredness is a major source of our discontent. Even if we display all the outward signs of happiness, we cannot be truly happy if we fail to take an interest in the happiness of others. Altruistic love and compassion are the foundations of genuine happiness.

These remarks are not intended to be moralistic; they simply reflect reality. Seeking happiness selfishly is a sure way to make yourself, or anyone else, unhappy. Some people might think that the smartest way to guarantee their own well-being is to isolate themselves from others and to work hard at their own happiness, without consideration for what other people are experiencing.

They probably assume that if everybody did that, we'd all be happy. But the result would be exactly the opposite: instead of being happy, they would be torn between hope and fear, make their own lives miserable, and ruin the lives of the people around them too. In the end, just "looking out for number one" is a losing proposition for everybody. One of the fundamental reasons such an approach is doomed is that the world is not made up of independent entities endowed with intrinsic properties that make them by nature beautiful or ugly, friends or enemies. Things and beings are essentially interdependent and in a constant state of transformation. The very elements that compose them only exist in relationship to each other. The self-centered approach of the ego continually runs afoul of this reality and only succeeds in creating frustration.

Altruistic love—also called loving-kindness—is the wish that others be happy and that they find the true causes of happiness. Compassion is defined as the desire to put an end to the suffering of others and the causes of that suffering. These are not merely noble sentiments; they are feelings that are fundamentally in tune with reality. All beings want to avoid suffering just as much as we do. Moreover, since we are all interdependent, our own happiness and unhappiness are intimately bound up with the happiness and unhappiness of others. Cultivating love and compassion is a win-win situation. Personal experience shows that they are the most positive of all mental states and create a deep sense of fulfillment and wholesomeness. Research in neuroscience also indicates that among all kinds of meditations, those focusing on unconditional love and compassion give rise to the strongest activation of brain areas related to positive affects. In addition, the behavior these forms of meditation give rise to is intended to benefit others.

If the deeds we perform for the sake of others are to have the intended benefit, they must also be guided by wisdom—the wisdom that we can acquire through analysis and meditation and that gives us a more correct understanding of reality. The ultimate reason for meditating is to transform ourselves in order to be better able to transform the world. To put it another way, we transform ourselves so that we can become better human beings and serve others in a wiser and more effective way. Meditation thus gives our life the noblest possible meaning.

A GLOBAL EFFECT

So the primary goal of meditation is to transform our experience of the world. In addition, studies have shown that meditation has beneficial effects our physical and mental health. For the last ten years, intensive studies on meditation and its long- and short-term effects on the brain have been conducted by major American universities, such as the University of Wisconsin in Madison, Princeton, Harvard, and the University of California at Berkeley, as well as research centers in Zurich, Switzerland—all inspired by the activities of the Mind and Life Institute, which is dedicated to the collaboration between Buddhism and modern science. In these studies, experienced practitioners who over time have meditated for between 10,000 and 60,000 hours demonstrated qualities of focused attention that were not found among beginners. For example, they were able to maintain more or less perfect concentration on a particular task for 45 minutes, whereas most people cannot go beyond 5 or 10 minutes before they begin making an increasing number of mistakes.

Experienced meditators are able to generate precise targeted mental states that are enduring and powerful. Among other things, experiments have shown that the region of the brain associated with mental states like compassion exhibits considerably greater activity among persons who have long meditative experience than among those who do not. These discoveries demonstrate that certain human qualities can be deliberately cultivated through mental training. Such studies have led to the publication of several articles in prestigious scientific journals, establishing the credibility of research on meditation, an area which had not been taken seriously until then. Richard Davidson, a leading neuroscientist, acknowledges: "These studies seem to demonstrate that the brain can be trained and physically modified in a way that few people would have imagined."[1]

Other scientific investigations have shown that you do not have to be a highly trained meditator to benefit from the effects of meditation: even 20 minutes of daily practice can contribute significantly to the reduction of stress, whose harmful effects on health are well established.[2] It also reduces anxiety, the tendency toward anger (which has been shown to diminish the chances of survival following heart surgery), and the risk of relapse for people who have previously undergone at least two episodes of serious depression.[3] Eight weeks of meditation (of the type known as Mindfulness-Based Stress Reduction, or MBSR)[4] for 30 minutes a day, significantly strengthens the immune system, reinforces positive emotions[5] and the faculty of attention,[6] reduces arterial pressure in those suffering from high blood pressure,[7] and accelerates the healing of psoriasis.[8]

To what extent can we train our mind to work in a constructive manner—for example, by replacing obsession with contentment, agitation with calmness, or hatred with kindness? Twenty years ago, it was almost universally accepted by neuroscientists that the brain contained all its neurons at birth and that their number did not change in adult life. We now know that new neurons are produced up until the moment of death. Moreover, scientists speak of "neuroplasticity," the brain's ability to continually change its structure and function in response to new experiences, so that a particular training, such as learning a musical instrument or a sport, can bring significant and lasting functional and structural changes in the brain. Mindfulness, altruism, and other basic human qualities can be cultivated in the same way. In general, if we engage repeatedly in a new activity or train in a new skill, modifications in the neuronal system of the brain can be observed within a month. It is essential, therefore, to meditate regularly.

Study of the influence of our mental states on our way of being and our health, which was once considered a purely eccentric notion, is now becoming a mainstream approach in scientific research.[9] The increasingly powerful Magnetic Resonance Imaging (MRI) techniques and sophisticated electroencephalograms (EEG) as well as magnetoencephalography (MEG), combined with the participation of experienced contemplatives, have led us toward a golden age of contemplative neuroscience. It is a fascinating prospect, and there is so much more to discover.

A fulfilled life is not made up of an uninterrupted succession of pleasant sensations but really comes from transforming the way we understand and work through the challenges of our existence. Training the mind not only makes it possible to cope with mental toxins like hatred, obsession, and fear that poison our existence, but also helps us acquire a better understanding of how the mind functions and gives us a more accurate perception of reality. This, in turn, gives us the inner resources to successfully face the highs and lows of life without being distracted or broken by them, and allows us to draw deep lessons from them.

One of the great tragedies of our time is that we significantly underestimate our capacity for change. Our character traits remain the same as long as we do nothing to change them, and as long as we continue to tolerate and reinforce our habits and patterns, thought after thought.

The truth is that the state that we call "normal" is just a starting point and not the goal we ought to set for ourselves. Our life is worth much more than that! It is possible, little by little, to arrive at an *optimal* way of being.

I cannot emphasize enough how much meditation and mind training can change our lives and bring about an inner revolution, which is profound and peaceful, and affects the quality of every moment of our experience.

Source of Inspiration

Unfortunately, one of the main obstacles we face when we try to examine the mind is a deep-seated and often unconscious conviction that "we're born the way we are and nothing we can do can change that." I experienced this same sense of pessimistic futility during my own childhood, and I've seen it reflected again and again in my work with people around the world. Without even consciously thinking about it, the idea that we can't alter our minds blocks our every attempt to try.

People I've spoken with who try to make a change using affirmations, prayers, or visualizations admit that they often give up after a few days or weeks because they don't see any immediate results. When their prayers and affirmations don't work, they dismiss the whole idea of working with the mind as a marketing gimmick designed to sell books . . . [However] during my conversations with scientists around the world, I've been amazed to see that there is a nearly universal consensus in the scientific community that the brain is structured in a way that actually does make it possible to effect real changes in everyday experience.

— YONGEY MINGYUR RINPOCHE[10]

Part II

WHAT TO MEDITATE ON

TRAINING THE MIND

The object of meditation is the mind. For the moment, it is simultaneously confused, agitated, rebellious, and subject to innumerable conditioned and automatic patterns. The goal of meditation is not to shut down the mind or anesthetize it, but rather to make it free, lucid, and balanced.

According to Buddhism, the mind is not an entity but rather a dynamic stream of experiences, a succession of moments of consciousness. These experiences are often marked by confusion and suffering, but we can also live them in a spacious state of clarity and inner freedom.

We all well know, as the contemporary Tibetan master Jigme Khyentse Rinpoche reminds us, that "we don't need to train our minds to improve our ability to get upset or jealous. We don't need an anger accelerator or a pride amplifier."[1] By contrast, training the mind is crucial if we want to refine and sharpen our attention; develop emotional balance, inner peace, and wisdom; and cultivate dedication to the welfare of others. We have within ourselves the potential to develop these qualities, but they will not develop by themselves or just because we want them to. They require training. And all training requires perseverance and enthusiasm, as I have already said. We won't learn to ski by practicing one or two minutes a month.

Refining Attention and Mindfulness

Galileo discovered the rings of Saturn after devising a telescope that was sufficiently bright and powerful and setting it up on a stable support. His discovery would not have been possible if his instrument had been inadequate or if he had held it in a trembling hand. Similarly, if we want to observe the subtlest mechanisms of our mental functioning and have an effect on them, we absolutely must refine our powers of looking inward. In order to do that, our attention has to be highly sharpened so that it becomes stable and clear.[2] We will then be able to observe how the mind functions and perceives the world, and we will be able to understand the way thoughts multiply by association. Finally, we will be able to continue to refine the mind's perception until we reach the point where we are able to see the most fundamental state of our consciousness, a perfectly lucid and awakened state that is always present, even in the absence of the ordinary chain of thoughts.

What Meditation Is Not

Sometimes practitioners of meditation are accused of being too focused on themselves, of wallowing in egocentric introspection and failing to be concerned with others. But we cannot regard as selfish a process whose goal is to root out the obsession with self and to cultivate altruism. This would be like blaming an aspiring doctor for spending years studying medicine before beginning to practice.

There are a fair number of clichés in circulation about meditation. Let me point out right away that meditation is not an attempt to create a blank mind by blocking out thoughts—which is impossible anyway. Nor is it engaging the mind in endless cogitation in an attempt to analyze the past or anticipate the future. Neither is it a simple process of relaxation in which inner conflicts are temporarily suspended in a vague, amorphous state of consciousness. There is not much point in resting in a state of inner bewilderment.

There is indeed an element of relaxation in meditation, but it is connected with the relief that comes from letting go of hopes and fears, of attachments and the whims of the ego that never stop feeding our inner conflicts.

A Mastery That Sets Us Free

As we shall see, the way we deal with thoughts in meditation is not to block them or feed them indefinitely, but to let them arise and dissolve by themselves in the field of mindfulness. In this way, they do not take over our minds. Beyond that, meditation consists in cultivating a way of being that is not subject to the patterns of habitual thinking. It often begins with analysis and then continues with contemplation and inner transformation.

To be free is to be the master of ourselves. It is not a matter of doing whatever comes into our heads, but rather of freeing ourselves from the constraints and afflictions that dominate and obscure our minds. It is a matter of taking our life into our own hands rather than abandoning it to the tendencies created by habit and mental confusion. Instead of letting go of the helm and just allowing the boat to drift wherever the wind blows, freedom means setting a course toward a chosen destination—the destination that we know to be the most desirable for ourselves and others.

AT THE HEART OF REALITY

Meditation is not a means of escaping reality, as some people think. On the contrary, its object is to make us see reality as it is, right in the midst of our experience, to unmask the deep causes of our suffering, and to dispel mental confusion. We develop a kind of understanding that comes from a clearer view of reality. To reach this understanding, we meditate, for example, on the interdependence of all phenomena, on their transitory character and on the nonexistence of the ego perceived as a solid and independent entity.

Meditations on these themes are based on the experience of generations of meditators who have devoted their lives to observing the automatic, mechanical patterns of thought and the nature of consciousness. They then taught empirical methods for developing mental clarity, alertness, inner freedom, altruistic love, and compassion. However, we cannot merely rely on their words to free ourselves from suffering. We must discover for ourselves the value of the methods these wise people taught and confirm for ourselves the conclusions they reached. This is not purely an intellectual process. Long study of our own experience is needed in order to rediscover their answers and integrate them into ourselves on a deep level. This process requires determination, enthusiasm, and perseverance. It requires what Shantideva calls "joy in virtuous ways."[3]

Thus we begin by observing and understanding how thoughts multiply by association with each other and create a whole world of emotions, of joy and suffering. Then we penetrate behind the screen of thoughts and glimpse the fundamental component of consciousness: the primal cognitive faculty out of which all thoughts arise.

LIBERATING THE MONKEY MIND

To accomplish this task, we must begin by calming our turbulent mind. Our mind behaves like a captive monkey who, in his agitation, becomes more and more entangled in his bonds.

Out of the vortex of our thoughts, first emotions arise, and then moods and behaviors, and finally habits and traits of character. What arises spontaneously does not necessarily produce good results, any more than throwing seeds into the wind produces good harvests. So we have to behave like good farmers who prepare their fields before sowing their seeds. For us this means that the most important task is to attain freedom through mastering our mind.

If we consider that the potential benefit of meditation is to give us a new experience of the world each moment of our lives, then it doesn't seem excessive to spend at least 20 minutes a day getting to know our mind better and training it toward this kind of openness. The fruition of meditation could be described as an optimal way of being, or again, as genuine happiness. This true and lasting happiness is a profound sense of having realized to the utmost the potential we have within us for wisdom and accomplishment. Working toward this kind of fulfillment is an adventure worth embarking on.

Part III

HOW TO
MEDITATE

Preliminary Instructions

Meditation is a matter not of theory but of practice, just as it does not satisfy your hunger to read a restaurant menu if you are not going to eat something from it. Nevertheless, it is an invaluable help to be able to consult the guidelines for meditation found in the works of the sages of the past. These works are treasure troves of instruction that clearly expound the goal and methods of meditation, describe the best way to practice it, and deal with the pitfalls that may await the practitioner.

Let us look now at some of these teachings. We'll begin with preliminary instructions and general advice, and then move on to some of the numerous methods of meditation. The descriptions will be kept simple so that these practices can be approached easily and gradually. Those who want to go into them more deeply will find references to more detailed works in the bibliography at the end of the book. The importance of an experienced living guide can never be overemphasized. It is not the intention of this book to replace such a guide. The aim is solely to provide some basic instruction derived from authentic sources.

A number of the exercises that follow, especially those dealing with mindfulness, inner calm, deeper insight, and altruistic love, are common to all schools of Buddhism. Others, for example those dealing with the emotions, come from the teachings of Tibetan Buddhism. Since this book is aimed particularly at readers who want to practice meditation without necessarily becoming Buddhists, certain essentials of Buddhist practice, such as "taking refuge" and other specifically Buddhist topics, will not be explained here. These can be found in fundamental texts including *The Words of My Perfect Teacher* by Patrul Rinpoche and the commentary of *Treasury of Precious Qualities* by Kangyur Rinpoche (Longchen Yeshe Dorje). In essence, let us remember that our mind can be our best friend or our worst enemy. Thus, liberating it from confusion, the self-centeredness of the ego, and afflictive emotions is the greatest favor we can do ourselves and others.

MOTIVATION

As with any other action, when we begin to practice a particular meditation, it is essential to be sure about our motivation. For it is our motivation—altruistic or self-centered, vast or limited—that will give the journey we are about to take a positive or negative direction and thus determine its results.

We would all like to avoid suffering and attain happiness, and we all have the basic right to fulfill these wishes. However, our deeds are in conflict with our aspirations most of the time. We look for happiness where it doesn't exist, and we rush headlong toward situations that make us suffer. Buddhist practice does not ask us to give up what is really good in life, but rather to abandon the causes of suffering, to which we are often addicted as if to drugs. Suffering is caused by mental confusion that dims our clarity and judgment. The only way to remedy this confusion is to develop an accurate view of reality and transform our minds. This is what will enable us to eliminate the primary causes of suffering: the mental poisons of ignorance, aggression, greed, pride, and jealousy, which in turn are caused by our self-centered and delusional attachment to the ego.

Buddhism speaks of several kinds of suffering. Visible suffering is evident everywhere, in the form of sickness, wars, poverty, disasters, and other overt sources of physical and mental pain. Hidden suffering is related to impermanence and change, and can conceal itself beneath the appearance of pleasure. An even deeper and less visible aspect of suffering comes from our basic ignorance and will stay with us as long as we remain in the grip of delusion and selfishness. Hidden suffering is related to impermanence and change, and can conceal itself beneath the appearance of pleasure. That is, even though we may be enjoying life, dramatic changes can occur suddenly: going to a nice picnic, for instance, and getting bitten by a deadly snake, or finding out that one has a serious illness. An even deeper and less visible aspect of suffering comes from our basic ignorance. As long as we remain in the grip of delusion and selfishness, afflictive mental states and emotions will continue to arise in the mind, triggering thoughts, words, and actions that are the causes of endless sufferings. From this perspective, a life lived in fundamental ignorance of the truth can never be truly happy.

Over 2,500 years ago, after attaining enlightenment under the Bodhi Tree, the Buddha gave his first teaching at a site known as the Deer Park outside Varanasi, India. There he taught the Four Noble Truths. The first is the truth of suffering, which needs to be recognized so that we don't remain endlessly and heedlessly under its spell. The second is the truth of the causes of suffering—in particular, the ignorance that engenders craving, hatred, pride, jealousy, and many other thoughts that poison our lives and those of others. Since these mental poisons can be eliminated, it is possible to put an end to suffering—the third truth. The fourth truth is that there is a path leading to the end of suffering. The path is a process that makes use of all available means to eliminate the fundamental causes of suffering.

But just getting rid of our own suffering is not enough. Each of us is only one person, while there is an infinite number of other beings—human and non-human who want to avoid suffering as much as we do. Moreover, all beings are interdependent, so we are intimately connected with every other living thing. So the ultimate goal of meditation is to acquire the ability to liberate all beings from suffering and contribute to their well-being.

Sections of this book under the heading "Meditation" contain concise and practical descriptions of various kinds of meditations. After reading these instructions, try to bring them into your experience during the meditation session, so that they become fully integrated in your mind and in your daily life.

The sections headed "Sources of Inspiration" throughout the book offer teachings and instructions spoken or written by great masters, which clarify, enrich, and deepen the various meditations proposed in the exercises.

Meditation: A Vow to Transform

Reflect on how you are now. Do you find patterns of behavior and habitual reactions in yourself that need to be improved or transformed? Look into the deepest part of yourself. Can you sense the presence of a potential for change there? Arouse the confidence to believe that change is possible through effort, determination, and wisdom. Take a vow to transform yourself not only for your own sake but also, and especially, for the sake of one day being able to dispel the suffering of others and contribute to their enduring happiness. Let this determination grow and take root in the deepest part of your being.

∽

Sources of Inspiration

Have we taken into account the overall situation or are we considering only specifics? Is our view short-term or long-term? Are we being short-sighted or clear-eyed? Is our motive genuinely compassionate when considered in relation to the totality of all beings? Or is our compassion limited just to our families, our friends, and those we identify with closely? Just as in the practice of discovering the true nature of our thought and emotion, we need to think, think, think.

— HIS HOLINESS THE 14TH DALAI LAMA[1]

May the precious Thought of Enlightenment
Be born in me if I have not already given birth to it.
Having been born, may it never wane
But always become greater.

— THE BODHISATTVA VOW[2]

CONDITIONS CONDUCIVE
TO MEDITATION PRACTICE

The Advice of a Qualified Guide

To start meditating, you must know how to go about it, and that is why a competent instructor is essential. In the best case he or she will be an authentic spiritual master who represents an inexhaustible source of wisdom and inspiration as well as many years of personal experience. In truth, nothing can replace the exemplary power and profundity of transmission from a living master. In addition to the master's inspiring presence and the teaching that he imparts constantly just by his way of being, he also makes sure that the student does not get sidetracked.

If you do not have the opportunity to meet such a master, you can benefit from the advice of a person who simply has more knowledge and experience than you do and whose instructions are based on an established contemplative tradition. If that is not possible either, the next best thing is to get help from a text, even a very simple one like the present book, which is based on trustworthy sources. That is preferable to putting yourself in the hands of a self-proclaimed teacher who has not received the transmission of an authentic lineage and whose advice is based on little more than his own idiosyncratic ideas.

A Suitable Place for Meditation

Our time and our minds tend to be taken up by all kinds of activities and preoccupations that never seem to end. That is why, in the beginning stage, we need to set up certain favorable conditions. Eventually the good effects of meditation will spread into our everyday life, especially through the practice of mindfulness, but to begin with, we need a protected environment in which to train the mind.

You don't try to learn the basics of navigation in the thick of a storm; you learn them in good weather on a calm sea. In the same way, it is best in the beginning to meditate in a quiet place where there is space for the mind to develop clarity and stability. Traditional Buddhist texts often compare this protected environment to an oil lamp. If a flame is continually exposed to the wind, its light will be weak and in constant danger of being blown out. On the other hand, if the flame is protected from the wind by a glass cover, it will be stable and bright. Likewise, if our mind is protected from distractions coming from the outside, mindfulness is given a better opportunity to be stable and clear, even though it will still have to contend with the inner distractions brought about by the wanderings of the mind.

An Appropriate Physical Posture

Your physical posture affects your mental state. If you assume a posture that is too relaxed, especially if you lie down, chances are that your meditation will stray into drowsiness. Too rigid and tense a posture, on the other hand, might lead to mental agitation. Thus it is appropriate to take a balanced posture that is neither too tight nor too loose. The texts recommend what is known as the "seven-point posture," also called the posture of Vairochana. These are the seven points:

1. The legs are crossed in the vajra posture, often called the lotus position. You begin by folding the right leg over the left, then the left over the right. If this is too difficult, you can use the half-lotus posture, also known as the tailor's pose, in which one foot rests on top of the opposite thigh and the other foot under the other thigh.

2. The hands rest palms up, on the lap in the posture of equanimity, with the right hand on top of the left and the tips of the thumbs touching each other. A variation is letting the hands rest flat, palms down, on the knees.

3. The shoulders are balanced, allowing a bit of space between the upper arms and the torso, so that the chest is open and relaxed and you can breathe freely.

4. The spinal column is quite straight "like a pile of gold coins."

5. The chin is tucked in slightly toward the throat.

6. The tip of the tongue touches the palate, near the front teeth.

7. The eyes are wide open or half closed, the gaze directed straight ahead or slightly downward, following the line of the nose.

If you have difficulty staying in a cross-legged position, then it is fine to sit in a chair or on a raised cushion on the floor. The essential is to maintain a balanced posture with the back straight, and follow the other posture points described above. It is said in the traditional texts that if the body is quite straight, the subtle energy channels will also be straight, and as a result, the mind will be clear.

Nevertheless, it is all right to modify your position slightly in accordance with the way your meditation is going. If you have a tendency to sink into apathy or even sleep, you can straighten your torso and adopt a more energetic posture while directing your gaze upward. If, on the contrary, your mind is too agitated, you can relax your posture a bit and gaze downward.

You should maintain a suitable posture for as long as you can, but if it becomes too uncomfortable, it is better to relax for a few moments than to be constantly distracted by pain. You can also, to the extent you are able, turn your attention directly to the experience of pain without either rejecting or amplifying it. Merely take it in as you would any other sensation, pleasant or unpleasant, as part of your mindfulness of the present moment. Also, you can alternate periods of sitting meditation with periods of walking meditation, a method that will be described later on.

Enthusiasm as the Driving Force Behind Perseverance

In order to have enough interest in something to devote time to it, you have to see its advantages. Contemplating the benefits that can be expected from meditation and then tasting them a little bit will nourish your interest. However, this does not mean that the practice of meditation is always pleasant. As Jigme Khyentse Rinpoche often says, "Meditation is not an entertainment." An expedition into the mountains is not always purely fun: along with wonderful moments in breathtaking landscapes, we may also face hardships such as rain, hail, exhaustion, altitude sickness, or losing our way. The essential point is to have enough interest in spiritual practice to keep going despite its ups and downs. The satisfaction of making progress toward the goal you have set yourself will then be enough to nourish your determination and sustain your conviction that the effort is worthwhile.

SOME GENERAL ADVICE

It is essential to maintain the continuity of meditation day after day, because in this way your practice gradually gains substance and stability. It is like the way a small trickle of water little by little turns into a stream and then a river. The traditional texts state that it is better to meditate regularly and repeatedly for short periods of time than to do long sessions every now and then. For example, you could devote 20 minutes a day to meditating formally and also take advantage of short breaks in your daily activities to recall the experience you had during your formal sessions, even if only for a few moments.

Short, repeated and regular sessions have a better chance of being high in quality than occasional long ones, and they will keep up a sense of continuity in your practice. For a plant to grow well, you have to water it a little every day. If you just pour a bucket of water on it once a month, it will most likely die between waterings. The same applies to meditation. This does not mean that you shouldn't occasionally meditate for longer periods if the opportunity arises.

If your meditation is too sporadic, there will be long periods during which you will fall back into your old habits and be overcome by negative emotions without being able to call on the support that meditation offers. But if you meditate frequently, even for short periods, it is possible to maintain a certain amount of your meditative experience between those formal sessions.

Being diligent in your practice should not depend on your mood of the moment. Whether your meditation session is enjoyable or irritating, easy or hard, the important thing is to persevere. If you get bored while meditating, this is not the fault of meditation itself but is due to your lack of training. Moreover, it is when you don't feel like meditating that it might have the most beneficial effects, because at those times meditation is working directly against some obstacle that stands in the way of your spiritual progress.

As we shall see later on when we look into this subject in detail, it is also important to keep your efforts balanced so that you don't become too loose or too tight. The Buddha had a student who was a great musician. He played the vina, a stringed instrument that resembles the sitar. This student had a lot of trouble meditating, and he questioned the Buddha about it. "Sometimes," he said, "I make an intense effort to concentrate, and then I become too tense and tight. At other times, I try to loosen up, but then I get too relaxed and fall into a sluggish state. What should I do?" In response, the Buddha asked him, "When you tune your instrument, what amount of tension do you put on the strings to make them sound the best?" The musician replied, "They have to be neither too tight nor too loose." The Buddha concluded, "It's the same with meditation. For it to progress harmoniously, you must find the right balance between effort and relaxation."

Practitioners are also advised not to place too much importance on various inner experiences that might arise during meditation. Such experiences might take the form of bliss, inner clarity, or an absence of thoughts. They can be compared to the different landscapes you see going by when you're sitting on a train. You would never consider getting off the train every time you noticed an interesting landscape, because the important thing is to keep going until you reach your destination. In the case of meditation, your goal is to transform yourself over the course of months and years. The progress you make is usually hardly noticeable from day to day, like the hands of a clock, which you barely see moving. You must be diligent but not impatient.

Haste and meditation do not go together; any profound transformation is bound to take time. It doesn't matter if the way is long; there's no point in setting a deadline. As the great Tibetan master Shabkar said, "The duration of your practice should be the duration of your life." The important thing is to know that you are heading in the right direction. Moreover, spiritual progress is not an all-or-nothing affair. Each step along the way, each stage, brings its measure of satisfaction and contributes to your development. In essence, what matters is not that you have an occasional transitory experience, but to see that you have undergone a genuine and lasting change after a few months or years of practice.

TURNING THE MIND TOWARD MEDITATION

In order to strengthen your determination to meditate, think about these four points:

1. The preciousness of human life

2. The fragility of human life and the transitory nature of all things

3. Choosing beneficial actions and avoiding harmful actions

4. The unsatisfactory quality inherent in ordinary life

THE PRECIOUSNESS OF HUMAN LIFE

If we enjoy conditions of freedom and opportunity, human life has extraordinary possibilities for inner development. Made use of intelligently, this life offers a unique opportunity to develop and actualize the potential we all possess but are so ready to neglect and fritter away. This potential, veiled by ignorance or mental confusion and by afflictive emotions, remains for the most part buried within us like a hidden treasure. The good qualities we acquire as we travel along the spiritual path represent the gradual emergence of this potential. This process has been compared to the cleaning of a gold nugget: once the dirt has been removed, it shines with dazzling brilliance.

Meditation: Precious Human Life

Realize how precious human life is and arouse a deep wish to draw out its quintessential qualities. Unlike the life of animals, human life offers an extraordinary opportunity to accomplish good things on a scale beyond that of your own personal existence. Your human intelligence is an extremely powerful tool that can create either great benefits or horrible disasters. Use it to achieve the gradual elimination of suffering and to discover genuine happiness, not only for yourself but also for those around you. In this way, every moment that passes will be worth living and you will have no regrets at the time of death, like a farmer who has cultivated his fields to the best of his ability. Remain for a few moments in the state of profound appreciation aroused by these contemplations.

THE TRANSITORY NATURE OF ALL THINGS

What is the use of reflecting on the transitory nature of beings and things? Human life has incalculable value, but it doesn't last forever. Reflecting on impermanence makes us realize the value of time. Each moment of life is so precious! Yet ordinarily we let it slip away like gold dust between our fingers. Why do we constantly put off until later what we intuitively know is of the highest importance? There's no point jumping up and down with impatience to get results as fast as possible, but we do need to develop an unshakable determination not to waste our time on distractions that make no sense. We must stop being taken in by the illusion that we have our whole life before us. Every moment of this life is precious, because death is certain and could occur at any time.

The way we think about death can exercise considerable influence on the quality of our lives. Some people are terrified by death, some prefer not to think about it, while others contemplate death in order to appreciate the value of each passing moment and realize that life is worth living. We are all equals in the face of inevitable death, but we differ in the way we prepare for it and in the way we go through it. The wise person relates to death as a helpful reminder that arouses courage and keeps him from useless distractions. He is not haunted by death, but he remains aware of the fragility of life. In this way, he gives full value to the time allotted to him. A person who takes advantage of every moment of life to become a better person, one who is better able to contribute to the happiness of others, can die in peace.

If we realize the fundamentally changing nature of all things, how can we believe that anyone is fundamentally good or bad, or that anything is permanently desirable or hateful? How can we perceive anything as intrinsically "mine"? How can we conceive of a permanent self in the midst of the constantly changing stream of our consciousness?

Understanding that change is inherent in the nature of all the animate or inanimate phenomena of the world keeps us from clinging to things as though they were going to last forever. Such an attitude of clinging will sooner or later translate into suffering because it is out of step with reality. Moreover, when change does happen, we will be less shocked because we will realize that change is in the very nature of things, and we will perceive it as less of an ordeal.

Meditation: Make the Best Possible Use of Time

Contemplate the passage of the seasons, of the days and months, of each moment, and the changes that affect every aspect of the life of beings. Then think about death, which is inevitable but whose time is uncertain. Who knows how much time you have left to live? Even if you live into old age, the latter part of your life will pass just as fast as the beginning, if not faster. So you need to consider, in the deepest part of yourself, what really counts in this life and use the time left to you to live in the most fruitful way possible—for your own sake and for others. If you have the wish to meditate and develop your inner qualities, it is never too soon to start.

∽

Sources of Inspiration

With all its many risks, this life endures
No more than wind-blown bubbles in a stream.
How marvelous to breathe in and out again,
To fall asleep and then awake refreshed.

— NAGARJUNA[3]

In the beginning, you should be pursued by
the fear of death like a deer escaping from a trap.
In the middle, you should have nothing to regret,
like a farmer who has tilled his field with care.
In the end, you should be happy, like someone
who has accomplished a great task.

— GAMPOPA[4]

CHOOSING BENEFICIAL ACTIONS AND AVOIDING HARMFUL ACTIONS

How can we make the best of this human life, which is precious but subject to being interrupted at any moment? If we want to carry out a plan or undertake some new activity, we have to be sure we are going about it in the right way. Certain things have to be done and others avoided. The sailor on the sea, the mountain guide, and the conscientious craftsman all know that nothing good comes from acting on the whim of the moment. This is even more true if the goal we are pursuing is to liberate ourselves from suffering. The intention here is not to set up good versus bad in some dogmatic fashion or to conform to some established convention.

Very simply, what we do have to do is behave with clear understanding and respect for the mechanisms of happiness and suffering that we ourselves can observe if we are attentive and insightful enough. It's as simple as realizing that if we keep our hand in the fire, there is no hope of escaping being burned. However, insisting on a 100 percent guarantee of the outcome of our choices is not a wise approach either. It is difficult to predict all the consequences of our deeds. But the least we can do—whatever activity we are involved in and whatever our circumstances may be—is to examine our motivation to be sure that our goal is not only of benefit to ourselves but also, and especially, of benefit to others.

Meditation: Distinguishing the Causes of Happiness and Suffering

Let your mind rest in its natural, uncontrived state and clear your thoughts. Recognize how deeply you wish to be free from suffering and to experience genuine happiness. Be intently aware that all living beings have the same wish. Reflect on the chains of causality that make certain types of thoughts, words, and actions—such as those inspired by hatred, greed, jealousy, or pride—result in suffering, and then on those other chains of causality arising from benevolence and wisdom, which lead to profound contentment. Take advantage of the wisdom of past teachers who have understood with great insight the mechanisms of happiness and suffering. Draw your conclusions about what you should or should not do, and arouse the determination to apply those conclusions in practice.

∞

Source of Inspiration

Beings long to free themselves from misery,
But misery itself they follow and pursue.
They long for joy, but in their ignorance
Destroy it, as they would a hated enemy.

— SHANTIDEVA[5]

THE UNSATISFACTORY QUALITY
INHERENT IN ORDINARY LIFE

We have already seen that our situation is far from satisfactory and that transformation is not only desirable but also possible. We can try to distract ourselves in many ways from the unsatisfactory aspects of life or to disguise them in all kind of attractive ways—for example, through engaging in constant activity, immersing ourselves in sensory experience, or pursuing wealth, power, and fame. But reality, with its inevitable measure of suffering, will always confront us in the end. For this reason it is better to look reality in the face from the start and resolve to uproot the actual causes of suffering and cultivate the actual causes of genuine happiness.

Meditation: Resolving to Change

For a few moments, be aware of your potential for change. Whatever your present situation is, evolution and transformation are always possible. At the least, you can change your way of seeing things and then, gradually, your way of being as well. Resolve deep within to liberate yourself from your present situation, and arouse the enthusiasm and the perseverance necessary to develop the good qualities that are latent within you.

∞

Source of Inspiration

Spending all your life trying to achieve ordinary worldly goals [like pleasure, gain, praise, and renown] . . . would be like trying to net fish in a dry riverbed. Clearly understanding this, make a firm decision not to allow your life to pursue such a useless course.

— DILGO KHYENTSE RINPOCHE[6]

MINDFULNESS MEDITATION

Our minds often get carried away with all kinds of thought associations in which dwelling on the past and projecting into the future are all mixed up. Distracted, scattered, and confused, we become remote from the immediate reality before us. We are hardly aware of what is going on in the present moment—the world around us, our sensations, or the way in which our thoughts multiply. In particular, we lose sight of the basic awareness that always lies behind these thought processes. Our automatic, mechanical thought patterns are the furthest thing from mindfulness. Mindfulness consists of full *awareness* of everything that arises within and around us from moment to moment—awareness of everything we see, hear, feel, and think. It also includes a correct *understanding* of the nature of our perceptions, free from the distortions that cause us to be attracted to or repelled by them. In addition, mindfulness contains an ethical component: it enables us to exercise *discernment* between states of mind that are beneficial and those that are harmful or pointless. These various components of mindfulness will enable us to decide which mental states should be phased out in the short and in the long term, and which wholesome mental states should be cultivated in order to achieve liberation from suffering.

The past no longer exists, the future hasn't arisen yet, and the present is paradoxically both ungraspable and unchanging. It is ungraspable because it never stays still, and it is unchanging because, in the words of the physicist Erwin Schrödinger, "The present is the only thing that has no end." Cultivating mindfulness does not mean that you should not take into account the lessons of the past or make plans for the future; rather it is a matter of living clearly in the present experience, which includes all three times.

Meditation: Observation Without Grasping

Observe what arises in your experience without imposing anything on it, without letting yourself be either drawn to it or put off by it. See whatever is in front of you, a flower or any other object; listen attentively to the sounds nearby or far away; smell the fragrances and odors; feel the texture of what you are touching. Register your various sensations, clearly perceiving their characteristics. Be entirely present to what you are doing, whether walking, sitting, writing, doing the dishes, or drinking a cup of tea. With mindfulness, it doesn't matter what you are doing or whether you judge a task to be pleasant or unpleasant. What matters is how you do it—with a mind that is clear and peaceful, attentive to what is happening, and full of wonder at the present moment, without superimposing mental constructs such as attachments or preconceptions onto reality.

When you are doing this practice, you stop endlessly swinging back and forth between attraction and aversion. You are just attentive, lucid, and aware of each perception and sensation, of each thought that arises and passes away. Feel the freshness of the present moment. Do you find that it brings up a vast, luminous, and serene state of mind in you?

∞

Source of Inspiration

When you hear a sound during meditation, pay attention to the experience of hearing. That and only that. . . . No mind movies. No concepts. No interior dialogues about the question. Just noise. Reality is elegantly simple and unadorned. When you hear a sound, be mindful of the process of hearing. Everything else is just added chatter. Drop it.

— BHANTE HENEPOLA GUNARATANA[7]

∞

Meditation: Mindful Walking

Here is an active approach to cultivating mindfulness that many people can use as a change of pace from sitting meditation. It consists of walking while concentrating totally on every step you take. You need to walk slowly enough to be able to be mindful of your least movement, but not so slowly that you lose your balance. With each step, be mindful of your balance, of how you touch your heel to the ground and then progressively bring your whole foot down, and of how the other foot leaves the ground and comes down again farther on. Keep your gaze directed downward a few steps in front of you, maintaining the walking itself as your main object of concentration. If you don't have a big space, then walk back and forth, pausing for a second or two each time you turn around and remaining mindful of this interruption of your movement.

∞

Source of Inspiration

Walking just for the pleasure of walking, freely and firmly, without hurrying. We are present in every step. When we wish to speak, we stop walking and lend all our attention to the person before us, to speaking and to listening. . . . Stop, look around, and see how wonderful life is: the trees, the white clouds, the infinite sky. Listen to the birds, delight in the light breeze. Let us walk as free people and feel our steps growing lighter as we walk. Let us appreciate every step we take.

— THICH NHAT HANH[8]

INNER CALM

The goal of meditation is to liberate the mind from ignorance and suffering. How do we do that? As we have seen, just wishing will not make it so. We have to apply a systematic method that will free our mind from the veils that obscure it. Since it is the mind itself that has to do the job, first we must prepare it properly. If it can't hold still for a minute, how can it free itself from its own ignorance? Earlier we used the analogy of a monkey. In this case the monkey is tethered by numerous ropes and keeps jumping around in all directions, trying to get loose. He jumps around so much that neither he nor anybody who wants to help him can untie a single knot. So the first thing that has to be done is to calm him down and make him pay attention. Calming the monkey doesn't mean tying him up and forcing him to keep still. The goal here is to take advantage of a moment of calm to free him. In the same way we must make use of the respite that comes when the mind is relatively calm and clear to free it from the bonds created by wild thoughts, conflicting emotions, and confusion.

The obstacles to attaining this goal are automatic thought patterns perpetuated by our habitual tendencies and the distractions and fabrications of the conceptual mind, which distort reality. We have to overcome these unfavorable conditions. Mastering the mind does not mean imposing an additional set of constraints on it that will make it even more tense and cramped than it already is. It means just the opposite—freeing the mind from the constraints of mental conditioning and inner conflicts created by dysfunctional thoughts and emotions.

So, in order to recognize the fundamental nature of the mind, we have to remove the veils created by automatic thought patterns. How do we do that? Suppose you are trying to retrieve a key that has fallen into a pond. If you poke about on the bottom with a stick, you'll completely muddy the water and won't have the slightest chance of spotting the key. The first thing you have to do is let the water settle until it becomes clear. After that, it will be easy to see the key and pick it up. We must work with our mind in the same way. We have to begin by making it clear, calm, and attentive. After that, we can use this new skill to cultivate other qualities, such as altruistic love and compassion, as well as to develop a deeper insight into the nature of mind.

Two basic, complementary types of meditation are practiced in all schools of Buddhism to attain these goals. One is *shamatha,* Sanskrit for "calm abiding"; the other is *vipashyana,* or "deeper insight." Shamatha is a peaceful state of mind, clear and perfectly concentrated on its object. Vipashyana is a deeper insight into the nature of the mind and of the phenomenal world. We acquire this deep insight first by detailed analysis of consciousness and then through contemplation, that is, through inner experience. Vipashyana allows us to see through illusion so that we can stop being a victim of afflictive emotions. In essence, shamatha prepares the ground by making the mind into a manageable tool that is precise and effective; vipashyana then liberates the mind from the burden of mental afflictions and the veils of ignorance.

Most of the time our mind is unstable, disorderly, and driven by whims as it bounces back and forth between hope and fear. It is self-centered, hesitant, fragmented, confused, and sometimes even absent, as well as weakened by internal contradictions and a feeling of insecurity. It rebels against any kind of training and is constantly occupied by a stream of inner chatter that generates a constant background noise we are barely aware of. Because these dysfunctional states are nothing but products of the mind itself, it makes sense that the mind can also remedy them. That is the object of practicing shamatha and vipashyana.

So the idea is to gradually progress from a state of mind where unfavorable conditions prevail, to another state that is characterized by stable attention, inner peace and clarity, confidence, courage, openness toward others, benevolence, the ability to deal with emotions, and other qualities of a vast and calm mind.

In the beginning, the practice of shamatha works to pacify the turbulence of our thoughts. In order to facilitate that, we sharpen our powers of concentration with the support of something we rarely pay any attention to—the coming and going of the breath.

Normally—unless we are out of breath from exertion or have been holding our breath—we are hardly aware of the coming and going of the breath. This is true despite the fact that breathing is virtually synonymous with being alive. Since our breathing just goes on by itself, if we can use it as a support for our concentration, we will have a tool that is precious because it is always available and, in addition, can serve as a reference point in gauging concentration or distraction.

This practice has three essential stages:

1. Directing our attention to a chosen object (in this case the breath)

2. Maintaining our attention on this object

3. Being mindful of the characteristics of the object[9]

Meditation: Mindfulness of the Breath

Sit in a comfortable position. If possible, adopt the seven-point posture described on pages 34–35, or at least a position in which your body is erect and well balanced. Here, mindfulness consists of remaining continuously aware of your breathing without forgetting it or letting yourself be distracted.

Breathe calmly and naturally. Concentrate all your attention on the coming and going of the breath. More specifically, focus your attention on the sensation created by the passage of air through your nostrils, the place where you perceive it most acutely. The precise spot varies from person to person: it might be at the opening of the nostrils, a little farther inside the nose, or higher up in the sinuses. Also notice the moment when breathing is suspended—between the out-breath and the following in-breath. After that, concentrate again on the point where you feel the breath passing. Then, also note the moment when the breath pauses for a moment, between the in-breath and the following out-breath.

Stay concentrated in the same way during the next cycle of breathing, breath after breath, without getting tense but also without relaxing to the point of falling into a sluggish state. Your awareness of the breath should be clear and calm. The Buddha gave the example of a cloud of dust raised by the wind: the dust was dispelled by a rain shower, giving way to a pure and brilliant sky. The dust here is the agitation and confusion of the mind; concentration on the breath is the saving rain shower; and the pure sky is calm and inner clarity.

Do not intentionally alter the rhythm of your breath. Your breathing will probably slow a little, but that should be allowed to happen naturally. Whether your breath is long or short, simply be aware of the fact that it is long or short.

Sooner or later, you will wander into a state of distraction accompanied by a lot of thoughts, or into a vague sleepy state, or even a combination of both—that is, into a state of confusion marked by erratic thought associations. It is at this point that vigilance has to be applied. As soon as you notice that you have lost your concentration, just resume it without adding to your distraction by feeling regret or guilt. Noticing that you have been distracted already marks the return of your mindfulness. Just come back to the breath, like a butterfly coming back to a flower after having fluttered around here and there for no apparent reason.

When thoughts appear, don't try to block them (which is not possible anyway, because they are already there); just avoid feeding them. Let them pass through the field of your awareness the way a bird passes through the sky without leaving a trace.

Occasionally, you may take the distraction itself as the object of your mindfulness. Then, once your mind has become attentive again, return your attention to the breath.

If other physical sensations appear, such as pain from sitting in the same position for a long time, do not struggle against the pain or become overwhelmed by it. Include it in your mindfulness, and then return to observing your breath. If the pain becomes so acute that it disturbs your meditation, it is a good idea to relax your position for a few moments or practice mindful walking for a short time. Then resume your meditation on the breath with a fresh mind and renewed concentration.

Variation 1: Counting Your Breaths

One method for reviving your concentration when it has become too weak is to count your breaths. For example, you can mentally count "one" at the end of a complete out-breath/in-breath cycle, then "two" at the end of the next cycle, and so on up to ten. Then begin again with one. This will help maintain your concentration.

If you prefer, you may count "one" at the end of an in-breath and "two" at the end of the following out-breath. This method and the ones that follow can be applied from time to time whenever it seems helpful, but it is not necessary to count your breath during your whole meditation.

Variation 2: Mentally Repeating Numbers

Another method is to mentally repeat "one, one, one, one . . ." fairly rapidly during the course of an in-breath, then "two, two, two, two . . ." in the same way during the course of the next out-breath. For the next cycle, count "three, three, three, three . . ." during the in-breath and "four, four, four, four . . ." during the out-breath. Count that way up to ten, and then start a new series.

Another possibility is to count rapidly from one to ten during the in-breath and then do the same during the out-breath. The object of these various ways of counting the breath is to refresh your concentration when it becomes sluggish or distracted.

Variation 3: Noticing the Movement of the Abdomen

Instead of observing the breath itself, you may concentrate on feeling the up and down movement of the abdomen that accompanies your breathing.

Variation 4: Mentally Repeating a Phrase

You can also associate a simple phrase with the coming and going of the breath. For example, while breathing out, you can mentally say, "May all beings be happy," and while breathing in, "May all their suffering be dispelled."

Variation 5: A Silent Mantra

Practitioners who recite mantras can combine silent recitation with attention to the breath. Thus with OM MANI PADME HUM,[10] which is the mantra of the Buddha of Compassion (Avalokiteshvara in Sanskrit), you say OM while breathing in, MANI PADME while holding the breath for a few seconds, and HUM while breathing out.

Variation 6: The Pause Between Breaths

In the normal instruction for this meditation, you should not influence the movement of the breath or slow down at the transitional point between in-breath and out-breath, but in this variation you concentrate for a few instants on the pause in breathing as the breath dissipates at the end of an out-breath. This is also the point at which discursive thoughts are suspended for a few instants. During this brief moment, rest in this clear bright space, calm and free from mental fabrications. You should not conceptualize this experience. Just recognize it is a basic aspect of your mind that is always present behind the curtain of thoughts.

These six variations can be practiced as you choose in order to improve your concentration.

THE FOUR FOUNDATIONS OF MINDFULNESS

The following meditations are intended to cultivate mindfulness and help develop a clearer understanding of the nature of mind and phenomena. You will successively focus your attention on your body, feelings, and mind and on phenomena at large (anything that you experience).

Meditation 1: Mindfulness of the Body

Adopt a comfortable, relaxed posture and direct your awareness to your body. When walking, be aware that you are walking; when standing, be aware that you are standing; when sitting, be aware that you are sitting; when lying down, be aware that you are lying down. Be aware of bending down or straightening up, bending forward or backward, lowering or lifting your head, eating, drinking, and so on.

You can also be mindful of your breath, as described earlier.

Then, concentrate on the various parts of your body, one after the other. Begin with your head, hair, ears, eyes, mouth, teeth, and so on. Send your attention down along your neck, shoulders, arms, hands, and fingernails. Move to the chest, to the waist, and down to the soles of your feet. Go up again.

Then visualize the inside of your body: the flesh, the tendons, the bones, the heart, the lungs, the veins and arteries and the blood running through them, the other bodily fluids, the liver, and the intestines. Focus your mindfulness on them.

Finally, simply place your awareness on whichever perception of the body arises in your mind.

Meditation 2: Mindfulness of Sensations

Whenever you perceive any feeling, whether pleasant, unpleasant, or neutral, simply embrace it with your awareness. Feel the breeze passing on your face or the point of contact of your feet with the ground.

If the feeling is pleasant, simply be aware of its pleasantness; if it is unpleasant, be aware of its unpleasantness. In the latter case, the sheer awareness of the unpleasantness replaces the reaction of repulsion that usually takes place. If you experience a diffuse feeling of your inner organs, concentrate on that. You may also concentrate on some parts of the body where you may not have any particular sensation at the moment, like your forehead or ears. Become aware of the subtle sense of their presence.

Finally, try to investigate the very nature of sensations. Aren't they just movements of the mind? Isn't it the same awareness that perceives them all, without being affected by them?

Meditation 3: Mindfulness of Mind

When thoughts arise, whether you try to suppress them or you follow after them and let them proliferate, you often feel overwhelmed by them. Instead, simply be aware of your thoughts and watch them like a spectator.

Whether your mind enters a state of craving, resentment or confusion, whether it is focused or scattered, dull or lucid, calm or agitated, be mindful of these states.

As will be explained later, you also need to understand the nature of these thoughts and find ways to free yourself from afflictive mental states.

Meditation 4: Mindfulness of Phenomena

Be fully aware of whatever enters the field of your experience and becomes an object for your mind: forms, sounds, odors, tastes, textures, thoughts, and emotions such as joy, sadness, desire, fear, irritation, dullness, and so on.

Whatever arises becomes a support for your meditation by providing an object of awareness. Watch how these phenomena appear, remain for a while, and vanish. Reflect on their transitory and illusory nature.

When your mind jumps from one phenomenon to another—sounds, forms, smells, and so on—and many thoughts flash through your mind in quick succession, if you remain mindful, the objects that attract your attention and thoughts themselves may change, but you will be able to achieve a continuous, all-pervading, panoramic mindfulness.

CONCENTRATION ON AN OBJECT

There are many other ways to cultivate concentration and mental calm. These methods are of two kinds—with or without an object of concentration. The object of concentration can be the coming and going of the breath, as described earlier, or other physical sensations, an emotion, a visualized image, or an external object. The external object can be a completely ordinary one, such as a small stone, a flower, or a candle flame. As with the breathing, the training consists in letting the mind rest attentively on the chosen object, bringing it back to this object when you notice you have become distracted.

The object can also be a symbolic or figurative image associated with a spiritual path, such as a painting or statue of the Buddha for those who practice the Buddhist path. You begin by concentrating on the external representation long enough so that all its details are present in your mind. Then concentrate on the mental image of the external representation. The following is the synopsis of an instruction given by Dilgo Khyentse Rinpoche.

Meditation: Visualizing an Image

Sit down and assume the seven-point posture. Let your mind calm down for a few moments, and then visualize Buddha Shakyamuni in the space in front of you. He is seated on a moon disk, which rests on a lotus and a throne held up by eight lions (not shown in simplified drawing on page 65). His body is resplendent, like a mountain of gold. With his right hand he touches the ground next to his right knee in the gesture of touching the earth (an iconic gesture representing the moment of his enlightenment, when he called on the earth to be his witness). His left hand rests in his lap in the gesture of equanimity, upon which rests a begging bowl filled with nectar. He wears the three monastic robes, and from his body emanates infinite rays of light and wisdom that fill the universe. Bring this image to life. Imagine that the Buddha you have visualized is not inert like a drawing or a statue. It is not made of flesh and blood either: his body is luminous and transparent like a rainbow, radiant with wisdom and compassion.

Try to concentrate one-pointedly on this complete visualization. You may then turn your attention to the details, to the perfect oval of the face, to the eyes filled with wisdom and love, to the harmoniously proportioned nose and ears, to the smile, and to the rays of light streaming out from the body. Progressively extend your concentration to all the details of the Buddha's form from top to bottom and from bottom to top, giving it the same level of meticulous attention a painter would give. Again, visualize the whole form of the Buddha, while retaining each detail as distinctly as possible

To reinforce your concentration, immediately neutralize anything that might disturb your mind. If your thoughts get agitated so that they keep you from developing a clear image, slightly lower your gaze (which normally rests in space) and concentrate on the lower part of the Buddha: the crossed legs, the throne held up by the lions, and the lotus seat. The effect of that will be to reduce your mental agitation.

If your mind falls into a state of sluggishness, slackness, or dull indifference, raise your eyes and concentrate on the upper part of the visualization: the Buddha's face, his eyes, the point between his eyebrows.

If your visualization is not clear, don't give up, but keep trying to get it more refined and precise. If it is clear, hold it in a natural way without tension.

When your mind becomes stable and peaceful, examine it. Realize that the image you are visualizing is not the Buddha himself but a projection of your mind whose goal is to help you cultivate concentration. Even though your mind has the ability to concentrate on an object, the mind itself cannot be found anywhere. It is impossible to locate the mind, to identify its shape, color, or form, or to see where it comes from, where it stays, or where it is going. You will never find anything. The mind is not an independent entity that can be identified as such.

The same is true of the body. What we call "the body" is simply a conglomeration of many elements put together. We give the name "heap" to a collection of grains, "sheaf" to a collection of dried straw, and "crowd" to a gathering of people, but none of these things are entities in their own right. Likewise, for this collection of things we call the body, if you take away the skin and the flesh, the marrow, the bones, and the different organs, once they have all been separated from each other, there is no other entity present that you can identify as "the body."

In fact, all phenomena in their infinite variety throughout the universe appear as a result of particular causes and conditions coming together temporarily. You take phenomena to be things that truly exist simply because you have not examined them properly. In truth, they have no solid, intrinsic existence at all.

When it becomes clear that your body, the image of the Buddha you are visualizing, and all phenomena are the display of the mind and that the mind's nature is not an entity endowed with independent existence but rather a dynamic stream of experiences, simply remain in the recognition of that nature without wandering. Remain attentive to whether or not thoughts interrupt this recognition. When thoughts arise, be aware of them without either hindering or encouraging them. This is what is called "deeper insight." It is essential to bring together mental calm (shamatha) and deeper insight (vipashyana) in this way.

∞

Source of Inspiration

Flawless *quiescence* [shamatha] is like an oil lamp that is unmoved by wind. Wherever the awareness is placed, it is unwaveringly present; awareness is vividly clear, without being sullied by laxity, lethargy, or dimness; wherever the awareness is directed, it is steady and sharply pointed; unmoved by adventitious thoughts, it is straight. Thus, a flawless meditative state arises in one's mind-stream; and until this happens, it is important that the mind is settled in its natural state.

— PADMASAMBHAVA[11]

CONCENTRATION WITHOUT AN OBJECT

At first, it might seem that meditation without an object would be easier than meditation with an object. But in fact, it is harder to keep your mind clear and concentrated on itself in a state of pure awareness than to concentrate on something. Concentration on an object implies a certain mental activity connected with attention, and even if it is hard to maintain this concentration, it is nevertheless easier than resting your mind in a state of perfect simplicity devoid of all mental constructs. That being said, you should know that concentration without an object is the natural culmination of concentration with an object and represents a further step in the understanding of the basic nature of the mind through direct experience.

Meditation: Awareness

Direct your mind inward and allow it to contemplate its primary quality, which is simply *knowing,* being aware. This faculty of awareness—which is mindfulness in its pure state—illuminates all thoughts and all perceptions. It is a constant and fundamental quality of the flow of consciousness. You can experience it even in the absence of thoughts and mental images. Try to identify this primordial aspect of all experience, and then let your mind rest a few moments in this nondual awareness that is clear, lucid, and devoid of concepts and discursive thoughts.

֍

Source of Inspiration

It is present as transparent, utter openness.
Without outside, without inside—
An all-pervasiveness
Without boundary and without direction.

The wide-open expanse of the view,
The true condition of mind,
Is like the sky, like space:
Without center, without edge, without aim.

— SHABKAR[12]

OVERCOMING OBSTACLES

All training requires effort, and any change naturally encounters resistance. In the case of training the
mind with nonconceptual meditation, there are various
obstacles that can slow your progress. Included among
the obstacles discussed in traditional instructions on
meditation are laziness and sluggishness, and their opposites, distraction and agitation, as well as the lack of
perseverance and its opposite, excessive effort.

Laziness and Distraction

Laziness, usually interpreted as indolence or lack of
motivation, can take several forms. Ordinary laziness is
the fault of shying away from any effort. Its antidote consists of recalling the preciousness of human existence and
of each passing moment, and contemplating the benefits
of inner transformation. Reflecting on those themes allows you to rekindle your inspiration and enthusiasm.

Another form of laziness is thinking, "That's not for me; it's beyond my abilities. I'd rather not get involved with it." In other words, you give up the race before you reach the starting line. To overcome this obstacle, give the potential for transformation that exists in you its true value and look at the purpose of your life on a larger scale.

A third form of laziness is not having the determination to do immediately what you know to be the most important thing and wasting your time instead on minor activities. To remedy this, establish priorities among your projects, and remember that, while your days are numbered, ordinary activities are like waves on the ocean—there is no end to them.

Distraction is the most common of meditation's enemies. What practitioner is not the victim of it? Distraction is completely normal at the beginning of practice, because your mind is undisciplined and chaotic, and you can't reasonably expect it to calm down immediately—so there is no reason to give up hope. The goal of meditation is precisely to make your mind smooth and manageable so that it can be concentrated or relaxed at will; and especially to free it from the tyranny of mental afflictions and confusion. The antidote to distraction is cultivating vigilance. Whenever you notice that your mind has wandered off, bring it back to the object of meditation. If you suddenly realize you have been distracted, it shows you have recovered your mindfulness, so you should be happy about this instead of being discouraged and regretful. The more often you notice that you have been distracted, the more your mindfulness is progressing. Remember also why you are meditating. Your goal is not to waste time giving free rein to your thoughts, but to use your meditation time to gain freedom from suffering.

Sluggishness and Agitation

Sluggishness and agitation are also major obstacles that make us lose the thread of meditation. Sluggishness, or laxity, undermines the clarity of the mind; agitation undermines its stability. Sluggishness can range from simple heaviness to sleep, with lethargy, irritation, daydreaming or other vague and blurry mental states in between. The mind withdraws and becomes excessively inward. This lack of clarity is a major obstacle precisely because you want to use your concentration to better understand the nature of the mind. As Bokar Rinpoche, a contemporary meditation master, explains: "When we look at the sea in the full light of day, we can see stones and algae on the bottom through the clear water. Meditation should have this same clarity, which allows us to be mindfully aware of the situation of our mind. By night, on the other hand, the surface of the waves is a dark and opaque mass that our vision cannot penetrate; in this same way a dim and heavy mind, in spite of an appearance of stability, is a hindrance to meditating."[13]

The advice for countering sluggishness is to adopt a more upright and energetic posture, to gaze slightly upward into the space in front of you, and to wear lighter clothing if you are too warmly dressed. You should also refresh your attention, putting emphasis on the mindfulness of the present moment.

Agitation is a hyperactive form of distraction in which the mind produces a chain of thoughts that is maintained by automatic patterns and imagination. This feverish agitation keeps transporting you far away from your object of concentration. Your body is sitting quietly, but your mind is off on a world tour. When this occurs, relax your physical posture a bit, lower your gaze, and come back to yourself by recalling why you are here and what the goal of your efforts is.

Lack of Perseverance and Excessive Effort

Any kind of training requires regular effort. A lack of perseverance considerably diminishes the effects of meditation and thus reduces its power to transform us. Again, a big occasional effort does not have the same beneficial effect as less spectacular effort that is more constant. Sporadic efforts will not be enough to transform the mind in a deep and long-lasting way. The remedy for this weakness is to reflect on the preciousness of the time that is passing, on the uncertainty of the duration of life, and on the benefits of the training you are engaged in.

By overdoing the remedies for laxity, you might temporarily fall into the opposite fault of excessive effort. The tension resulting from that also ends up as a distraction to your meditation. For this reason, you have to balance your efforts and find the happy medium between tension and relaxation, as the Buddha advised the vina player to do in the example given earlier. So stop applying a particular antidote when it is no longer necessary, and let the mind rest calmly in its natural state.

Excessive effort can also result from impatience or exaltation, two states that lead nowhere. If you begin climbing a high mountain at a run, your lungs will soon force you to stop. In the same way, if you draw a bow too far, it will break, or if you try to cook on too high a flame, you will end up burning your food.

Demanding immediate results is an aspect of unsteadiness of mind or laziness. His Holiness the Dalai Lama joked: "In the West, people would like enlightenment to be fast, easy, and if possible, cheap!" In the same way that it takes patience to grow a crop, steadiness is indispensable for the practice of meditation. It does no good to pull your plants to make them grow faster!

NINE METHODS FOR CULTIVATING ATTENTION

Traditional meditation texts teach nine methods to help establish the mind in a state of equanimity and make it more stable. Bear in mind that here we are talking about mindfulness in the sense of remaining continually attentive to a chosen object of concentration:

1. Focus your mind on an object, even if at the beginning it is only for a brief moment. Follow the meditation instructions and teachings you have received and avoid letting your mind be carried away by images and discursive thoughts.

2. Refocus your mind repeatedly, asking yourself again and again: Am I keeping my attention on the object? Bring the attention quickly back to its object as soon as you notice that distraction has caused it to stray. To do that, you first have to recognize

that your mind has been distracted, then identify the emotion or thought that caused this distraction, and apply the appropriate antidote. Little by little, you will develop the ability to keep your mind calm and stable for longer periods of time, and your concentration will become clearer and clearer.

3. Keep your mind on the chosen object continuously over a longer period of time, without falling into distraction. Focus on the various instructions for maintaining concentration on the mind's support given in the former sections. Recall those instructions and apply them with care. If you do this, you will be able to recognize distraction almost as soon as it occurs.

4. Direct your mind with care. The firmer your mind is and the more precise it is in its concentration, the more you will be inclined to meditate. Even if your attention is not yet perfect, you will reach the point where you no longer completely lose track of the object of meditation, and you will become free from the coarsest and most disturbing forms of mental agitation.

5. Master your mind. Even when your concentration becomes more stable, you might fall into a subtle form of sluggishness. When your concentration deteriorates in

this way, renew the sharpness and clarity of your awareness, and rekindle your inspiration and enthusiasm by considering the benefits of perfect concentration (samadhi).

6. Pacify your mind. Heightening your mindfulness to counteract subtle mental laxity may lead to subtle agitation. It can take the form of a little conversation going on in the background of your attention. When this occurs or your concentration becomes too sharp, simply consider the drawbacks of agitation and distraction. This will calm your mind and make it clear and transparent, like the pure sound of a well-tuned musical instrument.

7. Pacify your mind completely by using sustained and energetic attention. If meditative experiences arise, let go of attachment to them. These experiences may appear in a number of forms, such as bliss, clarity, or the absence of discursive thoughts. They can also take the form of spontaneous bursts of joy, unshakable confidence, fear, exaltation, discouragement, certainty or doubt, renunciation of worldly concerns, passion, intense devotion, or negative views. Any of these experiences can arise for no apparent reason. They are a sign of profound changes going on in your mind. It is necessary

to keep yourself from identifying with these experiences. Give them no more importance than you would to the flashing scenery you watch from a moving train. Perfectly pacified attention will cause these experiences to fade away without upsetting your mind. You will then know a profound inner peace.

8. Keep your attention concentrated on one point. After eliminating sluggishness and mental agitation, you will develop the ability to keep your attention stable and clear through an entire meditation session. Your mind will then be like an oil lamp protected from the wind, whose stable and bright flame gives out maximum light. A minimal effort at the beginning of the session will then be enough to establish the mind in the flow of concentration, where it can be maintained without difficulty, remaining in its natural state free from constraints and disturbances.

9. Rest in a state of perfect equilibrium. When your mind has become completely used to concentrating on a single point, it will remain in a state of equanimity that will arise spontaneously and perpetuate itself without effort.

DEVELOPING INNER CALM

Gradually your mind will calm down. However, just the opposite may seem to be happening. When you try to calm your mind, it may seem as if you have more thoughts than before. In fact, your thoughts have not really increased in number; it's just that you have become aware of how numerous they are. I have already pointed out that it is neither possible nor desirable to block thoughts. Yet it is important to gain some mastery over the thought process if you want to eliminate the causes of suffering and be able to develop genuine well-being. Allowing the mind to indulge in automatic, habitual thoughts only strengthens suffering, whereas meditating regularly leads to inner peace and freedom. Thus, far from inducing a stupor or destroying spontaneity, the disciplined practice of meditation gives us true mastery.

Buddhist texts illustrate the pacification of turbulent thoughts with the metaphor of a roaring waterfall that calms down gradually as its waters flow into the plains and finally run into the vast ocean. This meditative development occurs in five stages, portrayed in five images of water:

1. A waterfall tumbling from a cliff. Thoughts continuously add up and multiply. They seem more numerous than before because you are becoming aware of the movement of your mind.

2. A torrent hurtling through successive gorges. The mind alternates between periods of rest and activity.

3. A broad river flowing with few obstructions. The mind occasionally becomes agitated when it is disturbed by significant events, but otherwise it remains calm.

4. A lake ruffled by a few waves. The mind is mildly agitated on the surface but remains calm and clear in the depths.

5. A peaceful ocean. Concentration is now unshakable and effortless, so that you no longer need to apply antidotes against wandering thoughts.

Such a development is not accomplished in one day or even a few weeks, but sooner or later the moment comes when you see real progress. Everyone knows that it takes time and perseverance to master an art, a sport, a language, or any other discipline. Why should it not be the same with training the mind? It is a worthwhile adventure. We are not talking about acquiring some ordinary ability, but rather about a new way of being that will determine the quality of our entire life.

Source of Inspiration

At the beginning, nothing comes.
In the middle, nothing remains.
In the end, nothing goes away.

— MILAREPA

MEDITATIONS ON ALTRUISTIC LOVE

We have all, to varying degrees, had the experience of profound altruistic love, of a feeling of all-encompassing benevolence, of intense compassion for those who are suffering. Some people are naturally more altruistic than others, at times to the point of heroism. Others are more focused on themselves and find it hard to consider the welfare of others as an essential goal, and even harder to put the welfare of others before their own. In any case, it is essential to cultivate altruism. Being altruistic not only helps us to benefit others, but it is also the most satisfying way to live. This is the opposite of a heightened feeling of self-centeredness, which cuts us off from altruistic love and compassion and only brings pain to ourselves and others.

In general, even when altruistic thoughts arise in our minds, they are fairly quickly replaced by other, less wholesome thoughts, such as those of anger or jealousy. That is why, if we want altruism to play a major role in our being, we must spend some time cultivating it, because just wishing is not enough.

Earlier, we characterized meditation as a means of familiarizing ourselves with a new way of being. Now, how can we meditate on altruism? First of all, we must realize that in the deepest part of ourselves, we do not want to suffer; we want to be happy. Once we have recognized this aspiration, the next thing we must do is realize that all beings share it. We also need to realize that the right to be free from suffering, though often ignored, is without a doubt the most fundamental right of all beings. Finally, we must realize that there are causes and conditions of suffering, and therefore remedies for it.

Sadly, when it comes to choosing the means of creating happiness and preventing suffering, we are often unskillful or completely off the mark. Some people get lost on the wrong track by blindly pursuing their own happiness at the price of others' suffering. Generally speaking, we should wish wholeheartedly for all beings to be delivered from the causes of suffering. To this end, Buddhist texts advise us to cultivate four particular thoughts or attitudes and to extend them to all beings, in every direction, without limit. These are altruistic love, compassion, joy in the happiness of others, and equanimity.

Meditation 1: Altruistic Love

Imagine that a young child approaches you and gives you a look that is joyous, confident, and full of innocence. You stroke his head, look at him with tenderness, and take him in your arms. You feel a sense of unconditional benevolence and love. Let yourself be entirely pervaded by this love that wishes only for his well-being. Then cultivate, sustain, and nourish this feeling of loving-kindness. When it declines, revive it. At the end of the session, rest for a few moments in the mindful awareness of love.

You could also choose someone else toward whom you feel great tenderness and deep gratitude. Wish with all your heart that this person will find happiness and the causes of happiness. Then extend this wish to all those you are close to . . . then to those you know less well . . . then progressively to all beings.

Finally, extend this wish to your personal enemies and to the enemies of humanity. This last case does not mean you wish them success in their deadly plans. You are simply formulating a strong wish that they will give up their hatred, greed, cruelty, and indifference, and that benevolence and care for the happiness of others will be born in their minds. The worse an illness is, the more the sick person needs care, attention, and goodwill.

In this way, embrace the totality of beings with a feeling of limitless love.

Meditation 2: Compassion

Now imagine that someone dear to you has been the victim of a terrible accident. It is nighttime, and she is lying covered with blood on the roadside, suffering from terrible pain. Help is late in arriving and you don't know what to do. You feel this dear person's suffering intensely, as though it were your own, and this is mixed with a growing sense of distress and helplessness. This pain strikes you in the deepest part of your being, to the point where it becomes nearly intolerable. What should you do?

At this moment, let yourself enter an immense feeling of love toward this person.

Imagine taking her gently in your arms. Imagine that waves of love stream forth from you and pour over her. Imagine that each atom of her suffering is replaced by an atom of love. Wish from the bottom of your heart for her to survive, be healed, and cease to suffer.

This feeling of compassion comes from the same place in you as altruistic love and is that same love applied to those who are suffering.

Now extend this compassion to other people who are close to you, then, little by little, to all beings, making the following wish deep in your heart: "May all beings be free from suffering and the causes of suffering." This wish should apply not only to the obvious sufferings that we constantly witness in the world—sickness, poverty, famines, wars, death—but to the deeper, less visible causes of lasting suffering, mainly ignorance and the mental afflictions that ignorance brings about, such as hatred, craving, arrogance and envy.

Meditation 3: Joy in the Happiness of Others

Many people in this world have tremendously good qualities. There are those who lavish benefits on humanity and whose humanitarian projects have been crowned with success. There are also people who have realized their aspirations through great effort and steadfast perseverance, and still others who possess many talents.

Rejoice from the bottom of your heart in the accomplishments of these people. Wish for their good qualities not to wane, but on the contrary to continue and flourish. The ability to feel joy in the most positive qualities of others is the best antidote there is to discouragement and to a dim and desperate view of the world and of human beings. It is also the remedy for envy and jealousy, which are reflections of the inability to rejoice in the happiness of others.

Meditation 4: Equanimity

Impartiality is an essential element in the three preceding meditations, because the wish for all beings to be delivered from suffering and its causes has to be universal and not dependent on our personal bias or on the way others treat us. Take the point of view of a doctor who is willing to heal sick people no matter who they are or how seriously ill they are.

Realize that all beings—whether they are your dearest intimates, strangers, or enemies—want to avoid suffering. Also reflect on the fundamental interdependence of all the phenomena of the universe and of the beings who inhabit it. Interdependence is the very basis of altruism. Like the sun that shines equally on good and bad people, on beautiful landscapes or dung heaps, do your best to extend the altruistic love, compassion, and joy you cultivated in the three preceding meditations to all beings without distinction.

Recall again that when it comes to your own and others' enemies, you do not intend to encourage or passively tolerate their attitudes and harmful acts, but you look on them as very disturbed or deluded people. So, with the same goodwill that you feel toward those who are close to you, wish for all ignorance and destructive feelings to be eradicated from their consciousness.

Combining the Four Meditations

Begin with altruistic love, the strong wish for others to find happiness and the causes of happiness. If, after a while, this love drifts toward attachment, move on to the meditation on impartiality in order to extend your love and compassion equally to all beings—dear ones, strangers, or enemies.

If your impartiality turns into indifference, it is time to think of people who are suffering and arouse intense compassion within yourself, with the wish to relieve these beings from all their suffering. But it may happen that, as a result of being continually concerned with the endless misfortunes of others, you may be overcome by a feeling of depression and helplessness, even despair, to the point where you feel overwhelmed by the immensity of the task and lose heart. At that point meditate on your joy in the happiness of others, thinking of those people who possess great human qualities and of those whose altruistic aspirations have been successful. Rejoice fully in that.

If that joy turns into blind euphoria and distraction, return again to altruistic love—and so on. Develop the four thoughts in this way while avoiding the pitfalls possible in each of them.

At the end of your meditation, contemplate the interdependence of all things for a few moments and their lack of autonomous, intrinsic existence. Understand that, just as a bird needs two wings to fly, you must develop wisdom and compassion simultaneously. Wisdom is a correct understanding of reality and compassion is the desire for all beings to be liberated from the causes of suffering.

∞

Sources of Inspiration

Compassion . . . is a spontaneous feeling of connection with all living things. What you feel, I feel; what I feel, you feel. There's no difference between us. . . . When I began to practice meditation on compassion, however, I found that my sense of isolation began to diminish, while at the same time my personal sense of empowerment began to grow. Where once I saw only problems, I started to see solutions. Where once I viewed my own happiness as more important than the happiness of others, I began to see the well-being of others as the foundation of my own peace of mind.

— YONGEY MINGYUR RINPOCHE[14]

May I be a guard for those who are protectorless,
A guide for those who journey on the road.

For those who wish to cross the water,
May I be a boat, a raft, a bridge.

May I be an isle for those who yearn for land,
A lamp for those who long for light;
For all who need a resting place, a bed;
For those who need a servant, may I be their slave.

May I be the wishing jewel, the vase of wealth,
A word of power and the supreme healing,
May I be the tree of miracles,
For every being the abundant cow.

Just like the earth and space itself,
As far as are the limits of the sky,
For boundless multitudes of beings,

May I always be the ground of life,
the source of varied sustenance.
Thus for everything that lives,
As far as are the limits of the sky,

May I be constantly their source of livelihood
Until they pass beyond all sorrow.

— SHANTIDEVA[15]

And now as long as space endures,
As long as there are beings to be found,
May I continue likewise to remain
To drive away the sorrows of the world.

— SHANTIDEVA[16]

A SUBLIME
EXCHANGE

Profound suffering can sometimes awaken our hearts and minds, and open them to others. There is a particular practice whose purpose is to turn this opening into a lasting state. It consists of mentally exchanging the suffering of others for our own happiness, and also wishing that our own suffering may substitute for the suffering of others. This is done through the vehicle of the breath.

Perhaps we think we have enough problems already and it's asking too much to add to our burden by taking on the suffering of others. However, what happens as a result of this practice is just the opposite. Experience shows that when we mentally take on, transform, and dissolve the suffering of others through compassion, not only does that not increase our own suffering but it dispels it. The reason for this is that altruistic love and compassion are the most powerful antidotes there are to our own pain. So this is a situation where everybody wins! On the other hand, self-centered dwelling on our suffering, reinforced by the constant refrain of "me, me, me" that it causes to resonate in our head, undermines our courage and increases our distress. But by breaking the spell of our self-centeredness, altruistic contemplation of the suffering of others greatly enhances our compassionate courage and our resolve to dispel their suffering.

This practice of exchange is a particularly effective means of developing altruism and compassion through meditation. As a result, when we actually come face to face with the suffering of others, we will be naturally inclined to behave in a compassionate manner and offer to help.

Meditation: The Practice of Exchange

Begin by feeling a strong sense of altruistic love toward a person who has been very good to you—your mother, for example. Think about her kindness. She gave you life after having gone through the difficulties of pregnancy and the pains of childbirth. As you grew up, she took care of you without sparing her strength. She put your happiness before her own and was always ready to sacrifice everything for you.

In order to arouse strong compassion, imagine that your mother is undergoing intense suffering, that she lacks the things she needs, that she is dying of hunger and thirst and is being treated badly. Imagine other painful situations she is facing. You can do this for any person you have chosen as the object of your meditation. It could be a child, a loyal friend, or an animal that you love. You could also imagine, for example, a doe pursued by hunters and their pack of dogs. Cornered and filled with panic, she jumps off a cliff and breaks her bones. The hunters find her dying and finish her off with their knives.

Picture all kinds of suffering in your mind with graphic precision. Imagine old or sick people suffering from the agonies of disease, poor people who barely have enough to live on. Think of those who have been deprived of everything they need and also of people who are victims of their own minds and are being driven mad by desire or hatred.

Do not forget to include in your love and compassion all those people you consider to be your enemies and who cause you trouble. Visualize in front of you all humanity gathered into an immense crowd and recall that, like you, they have suffered in many ways through an infinite cycle of lifetimes.

When an intense feeling of compassion arises, begin the practice of exchange. Think that as you breathe out, along with your breath you send out to those who are suffering all your happiness, your vitality, your good fortune, your health, and so on, in the form of refreshing and radiant white nectar. Imagine that you give them these benefits without any reserve and that this nectar fulfills all their needs. If their life is in danger, imagine it is prolonged; if they are poor, imagine they receive whatever they need; if they are sick, imagine they are healed; and if they are miserable, imagine they find happiness.

As you breathe in, imagine you are taking upon yourself, in the form of a dark mass, all the illness, physical and mental problems, and the emotional disturbances of these beings, and that this exchange relieves their torments. Imagine their suffering comes back to you like a mist blown by the wind. When you have absorbed, transformed, and eliminated all their pain and trouble, feel a great joy, mixed with a feeling of nonattachment.

Repeat this practice many times until it becomes second nature. Never think you have done enough for those who are suffering.

This method can be applied at any time in any circumstances, and in particular when you yourself are suffering. In this case, generating altruism and compassion opens your heart to other people instead of letting your pain push you deeper into self-centered distress. As a bonus, it also acts like a soothing balm for your own pain. You can do this exercise at any time, in and out of meditation sessions, and apply it to all activities of your daily life.

Variation 1

As you breathe out, think that your heart is a brilliant shining sphere from which rays of white light stream out, bringing happiness to all beings in all directions.

As you breathe in, take in the torments of all beings in the form of a dense, dark cloud that penetrates into your heart and dissolves into a mass of white light without leaving a trace.

Variation 2

Imagine that your body multiplies itself into an infinite number of forms that reach the far ends of the universe, taking on all the suffering of all beings they encounter and offering them their happiness. Then your body transforms into clothing for those who are cold, into food for those who are hungry, and into a refuge for those who are homeless. Then you become a "wish-fulfilling gem," somewhat larger than your body and sparkling like a magnificent blue sapphire that naturally satisfies all the needs of anyone.

This practice allows you to associate your breathing with the development of compassion. It is very simple and can be used at any moment in your daily life—when you are sitting on a train, waiting in line or in a traffic jam, or whenever you are enjoying a break from your everyday activities.

SOOTHING
PHYSICAL PAIN

Physical pain is an experience we all have to face. But the subjective reaction we have to it varies significantly from person to person. The sensation of pain, for example, can be made much worse when we anticipate it or anxiously try to suppress it. At such a moment the mildest of pains can become intolerable. Chronic pain can be made much more bearable by changing our attitude toward it and imbuing it with some meaning.

Studies in neuroscience have shown that the way we evaluate pain can be modulated by our anticipation of it and depends to a great extent on the way our mind deals with it. We have more tolerance for pains that have a predictable duration and intensity. Predictability helps us to be ready for them when they arise. Thus, we can manage them better than pains whose intensity is subject to uncontrollable changes and whose duration is unknown. If pain gets completely out of control and we think it might last indefinitely, then our mind might easily be completely overwhelmed by suffering.

Another point is that giving pain a meaning helps us to bear it. We accept the painful secondary effects of a medical treatment we hope will cure us. We might also be willing to experience pain for the sake of helping another person. This is the case when a parent or friend gives blood or donates an organ to save the life of a dear one. The same goes for the pain, sometimes quite intense, that athletes endure in their training. They fully accept the pain because it results in improving their performance. Some athletes say that the more intense the pain is, the more they appreciate it as feedback on the intensity of their training. These same athletes report that they are much more negatively affected by unforeseen pain that has no value for them: for example, an injury that occurs in the course of their training. Bestowing a meaning on pain gives us power over it and does away with the anxiety that comes with feelings of confusion and helplessness. By contrast, if we react with fear, resentment, discouragement, lack of understanding, or a feeling of helplessness, then instead of just experiencing one pain, we add several more pains to it.

The most difficult cases are those of chronic, intense, and persistent pain that overpowers our other sensations. Such pain dominates the mind and our relation to the world; it accompanies our every thought and deed. I once heard a sick person say: "Intense chronic pain is like a stone thrown into a pond: its waves spread throughout your life. There's no place to run from it." All the same, we can suffer intense pain without letting it destroy our positive vision of life. If we are able to attain a certain level of inner peace, it is easier to maintain our strength of mind or to regain it quickly even when we are confronted by difficult circumstances.

People who have lived through an accident, torture, or other kinds of intense pain have indicated that later on they felt "more human" than before. They felt a deeper appreciation for the world around them, for the beauty of nature, and for the good qualities of the people they met. They said they considered every moment of their lives a priceless treasure.[17]

So how can we manage our pain rather than being the victim of it? If you cannot escape it, it is better to make use of it than try to resist it. Whether you fall into the deepest of depressions or maintain your strength of mind and your will to live, either way the pain will be there. In the second case, you will be able to preserve your dignity and self-confidence. That makes a big difference.

Buddhism teaches different methods for achieving this. I will explain four of them. The first consists in simply observing the pain mindfully, without interpreting it. The second makes use of mental imagery. The third allows us to transform the pain by awakening love and compassion. The last involves examining the nature of the suffering and, by extension, the nature of the suffering mind.

Meditation 1: Mindfulness of Pain

As explained in the quotations that follow, observe with pure mindfulness the sensation of pain without interpreting, rejecting or fearing it. Immerse yourself in the mindfulness of the present moment. Your sensation will then retain its intensity but lose its repellent character.

Most of us regard pain as a threat to our physical well-being. On one hand, when we worry or allow ourselves to become preoccupied by this threat, the pain itself almost always increases. On the other hand, if we consider pain or discomfort as an object of meditation, we can use such sensations to increase our capacity for clarity.

— YONGEY MINGYUR RINPOCHE[18]

How does one work with pain as an object of meditation? A pure unobstructed awareness of the pain will experience it simply as a flowing pattern of energy and nothing more. No thought and no rejection. Just energy . . . But the human mind conceptualizes such occurrences as "the pain." That is a concept. It is a label, something added to the sensation itself. You find yourself building a mental image . . . you will probably find yourself thinking [something like], "I have a pain in my leg." "I" is a concept. It is something extra added to the pain experience.

When you introduce "I" into the process, you are building a conceptual gap between the reality and the awareness viewing that reality. Thoughts such as "me," "my," or "mine" have no place in direct awareness. They are extraneous addenda, and insidious ones at that. When you bring "me" into the picture, you are identifying with the pain. That simply adds emphasis to it. If you leave "I" out of the operation, pain is not painful. It is just a pure surging energy flow.

— BHANTE HENEPOLA GUNARATANA[19]

Meditation 2: The Power of Mental Imagery

Visualize that a soothing, warm, and luminous nectar penetrates the place where the pain is at its worst, dissolves it little by little, and finally transforms it into a sensation of well-being. This nectar fills your entire body, and the painful sensation fades away. If the pain increases in intensity, then increase the strength of the nectar accordingly, thinking that each atom of pain is now replaced by an atom of well-being. In this way, transmute the very essence of the pain into bliss.

Meditation 3: The Force of Compassion

Arouse a powerful feeling of altruistic love and compassion toward all beings, and think: "I wish so much to put an end to my suffering. But others besides myself are tormented by pain that is comparable to my own or even worse. How I wish that they too could be liberated from their pain." You could also imagine that you have deliberately volunteered to experience pain to spare someone else—your child, for instance—from enduring it. Then your pain will no longer be perceived as something degrading or overwhelming. Filled now with altruistic love, you stop asking yourself bitterly, "Why me?" but rejoice that someone else has been spared that suffering.

When you are totally absorbed in yourself, you are vulnerable and an easy prey to confusion and feelings of distress, helplessness, and anxiety. If, instead of that, you feel a strong sense of empathy, combined with unconditional love toward the suffering of others, resignation will be replaced by courage, depression by love, and meanness by openness toward the people around you.

Meditation 4: Contemplating
the Nature of the Mind Itself

Contemplate the nature of pain. Even if it is sharp and penetrating, ask yourself what color is it, what shape is it, what other unchangeable characteristics it might have. With this kind of inquiry, the characteristics of the pain get blurry the minute you try to focus on it. You will soon recognize that behind the pain there is a pure awareness, the very same awareness that is at the source of any other sensation or thought. Relax your mind and try to let the pain rest within this pure awareness, free from any mental constructs. By taking this approach, you are no longer just the passive victim of the pain, and little by little you will be able to face it and overcome the bruising negative effects it has on your mind.

This last approach is certainly not easy, but experience shows that it is possible. I have known a number of meditators who have applied this method in the course of particularly painful terminal illnesses. They seemed remarkably calm and relatively little affected by the pain. My dear friend Francisco Varela, a well-known researcher in the cognitive sciences who had practiced Buddhist meditation for years, told me a few weeks before his death from an extensively metastasized cancer that he was able to remain almost constantly in a pure state of awareness. Then his physical pain seemed remote and did not interfere with his inner peace. He needed only weak doses of painkillers and was able to maintain his lucidity and serenity until his last breath.

DEEPER INSIGHT

Now let's explore another meditation practice, known as deeper insight (*vipashyana* in Sanskrit, *vipassana* in Pali). The way we perceive others and the world in general considerably influences our behavior and the way we live. We constantly impose a narrow view of reality on the world, and the resulting distortions turn into causes of frustration and suffering, because they inevitably clash with reality. How often have we decided that somebody or something was totally desirable or detestable? Taken in by the seeming solidity of these concepts, we cling to "me" and "mine" with tremendous tenacity.

Imagine you perceive the world of phenomena as a dynamic flow of interdependent events. You recognize that things are constantly changing simply because the causes and conditions that produce them are constantly changing, and that phenomena possess no intrinsic qualities of their own. The concepts of "me" and "mine" will now appear to you much more fluid and will no longer be the source of such powerful fixations.

Cultivating deeper insight in this way is an essential practice for rooting out suffering and the fundamental misunderstandings that are the source of it.

To develop deeper insight, it is absolutely necessary to have a clear, concentrated, and stable mind. That is why it is important to prepare the mind by practicing shamatha, or inner calm. Shamatha enables us to calm afflictive emotions temporarily, but by itself it is not enough to eradicate them completely. We therefore need to practice deeper insight as well. This will help us to recognize the basic nature of consciousness, the way emotions arise and become entangled with each other, and how our mental fabrications reinforce the self-centeredness of the ego. Deeper insight will allow us to understand—first through analysis and then through direct experience—that phenomena are impermanent and interdependent, and thus do not have the tangible, independent existence that is ordinarily attributed to them. The result of this will be greater truth and freedom in the way we perceive the world. We will no longer be prisoners of our self-centered vision. We will be better able to cope with the emotional reactions that arise as we interact with our surroundings.

Vipashyana can be practiced at different levels and in different ways. Let us examine several aspects of it here:

- How to arrive at a more accurate understanding of reality

- How to free ourselves from the torments of afflictive emotions

- How to unmask the deceptions of the ego and the consequences of grasping at the notion of an independent self, and understand their influence on our suffering and well-being

- How to understand the fundamental nature of the mind

UNDERSTANDING REALITY

What do I mean by reality? According to Buddhism, reality means the real nature of things, unmodified by mental fabrications, which create a discrepancy between the way things appear to us and the way they really are. This discrepancy is the source of continual conflicts with our world. Usually we perceive the external world as a composite of independent entities to which we attribute characteristics that seem to be an inherent part of them. Thus things appear to us as intrinsically "nice" or "not nice" and people as basically "good" or "bad." The "I," or the ego, that perceives all this also seems real and concrete to us. This misunderstanding, which Buddhism refers to as ignorance, brings about the powerful reflexes of attachment and aversion, which in turn lead to an endless succession of painful experiences.

According to Buddhist analysis, the world is a result of the coming together of an infinite number of causes and conditions that are continually changing. Just as a rainbow is formed at the precise moment the sun shines on a collection of raindrops, and disappears as soon as the factors that produce it are no longer present, phenomena exist in an essentially interdependent mode and have no permanent, independent existence. Ultimate reality is therefore described as "empty" of independently existing animate or inanimate phenomena. Everything is relationship; nothing exists in and of itself.

Once this essential idea has been understood and assimilated, our erroneous perception of our ego and our world gives way to wisdom—an accurate view of the nature of things and beings. Wisdom is not a simple intellectual construction or a compilation of information. It arises from a precise methodology that allows us progressively to eliminate mental blindness and the afflictive emotions that derive from it, and in that way free us from the principal cause of suffering.

The goal of the following meditation is to transform our perception of reality. It is described in contemporary terms, but it is based on a classical Buddhist philosophical analysis.[20]

Meditation: Investigating a Rose

Imagine a fresh rose that has just bloomed. It is so beautiful! Now imagine that you are a small insect nibbling on one of its petals. It tastes so good! Now imagine yourself as a tiger standing before this rose. For him, it makes no difference whether it is a flower or a bale of hay. Now transport yourself into the heart of this rose and imagine yourself as an atom there. You no longer exist except as pathways of energy in a kaleidoscopic universe, amid a whorl of particles passing through nearly empty space. Where did the rose go? Where are its color, form, texture, fragrance, and taste—where is its beauty? As for the particles, if you look at them closely, are they solid objects? Not really, the physicists say. They are events arising in the quantum void; they are "waves of probability" and, ultimately, of energy. Energy? Is that an entity? Isn't it more like a potential for manifestation that neither exists nor doesn't exist? What is left of the rose?

☽

Sources of Inspiration

Like a flickering star, a mirage or a flame,
Like a magical illusion, a dewdrop, or a bubble on a
stream, Like a dream, a flash of lightning, or a cloud,
See all compounded things as being like these.

— BUDDHA SHAKYAMUNI,
THE DIAMOND SUTRA

Like reflections on the surface of a clear lake,
The multitude of phenomena manifests,
Completely devoid of inherent existence.
This very day, acquire the certitude
That everything is no more
than reflections of emptiness.

— LONGCHEN RABJAM[21]

Subject and object are like sandalwood and its fragrance. Samsara and nirvana are like ice and water. Appearances and emptiness are like clouds and the sky. Thoughts and the nature of the mind are like waves and the ocean.

— GESHE CHAYULPA[22]

Lakes and rivers can freeze in winter and the water can become so solid that people, animals, and carts travel back and forth on its surface. At the approach of spring, the earth warms up and the waters thaw. What remains then of all that solid ice? Water is soft and fluid, ice hard and sharp. We cannot say that they are identical, but neither are they different—ice is only frozen water, and water is only melted ice.

It is the same with our perceptions of the external world. To be attached to the reality of phenomena, tormented by attraction and repulsion, and obsessed by the eight worldly preoccupations[23] is what causes the mind to freeze. Melt the ice of your concepts so that the fluid water of free perception can flow.

— DILGO KHYENTSE RINPOCHE[24]

Recognition of the nature of the mind and an accurate understanding of the phenomenal world are essential for our quest for happiness. If the mind relies on totally erroneous views about the nature of things and maintains them, it will be very difficult for us to transform ourselves and achieve freedom. Developing a correct view is not a question of faith or adherence to dogma but of clear understanding. This arises from a correct analysis of reality. Through this, little by little, the belief in the inherent existence of things, in which our erroneous conception of the world is rooted, is cast into doubt and replaced by an accurate view of phenomena.

— HIS HOLINESS THE 14TH DALAI LAMA[25]

DEALING WITH THOUGHTS AND EMOTIONS

Some people think that the aim of Buddhism in general and meditation in particular is to suppress the emotions. Whether this is true or not depends on what we mean by emotion. If we are talking about mental disturbances such as hatred and jealousy, why not get rid of those emotions? We sometimes hear the criticism that Buddhism views emotions as undesirable. Whether there is any truth to this depends on what emotions the critics mean. If they are talking about mental disturbances such as hatred and jealousy, Buddhism does see eliminating those negative emotions as a desirable goal—who wouldn't want to get rid of them? If they are talking about altruistic love or compassion for those who are suffering, these are indeed one of the goals of meditation; Buddhists certainly don't want to be emotionally indifferent toward others. If we are talking about powerful altruistic love or about compassion for suffering beings, why not develop these qualities? These are indeed the goals of meditation.

Meditation teaches us how to deal with bursts of malicious anger or jealousy, with waves of uncontrolled desire and irrational fears. It frees us from the tyranny of mental states that obscure our judgment and are the source of constant distress. Buddhism speaks of the afflictive emotions as mental "poisons," because these mental states truly poison our existence and that of others.

The word *emotion* comes from the Latin *emovere*, which means "to set in motion." An emotion is thus what sets the mind in motion, whether that motion takes the form of harmful, neutral, or wholesome thoughts. Emotion conditions the mind and leads it to adopt a certain perspective, a certain view of things. This view can be in accord with reality, as in the case of altruistic love and compassion, or distorted, as in the case of hatred or craving. As we have seen, altruistic love is an awareness of the fact that all beings wish, as we do, to be free from suffering. It is based on recognizing the basic interdependence of all beings. By contrast, hatred distorts reality by exaggerating the faults of its object and ignoring that object's good qualities. In the same way, avid desire makes us perceive its object as desirable from every point of view and ignore its faults.

Certain emotions both disturb the mind and obscure it, and can therefore be considered "mental afflictions" (often called "afflictive emotions" in Buddhism, a translation of the Sanskrit *klesha*); other emotions are beneficial. If an emotion strengthens our inner peace and encourages us to seek the welfare of others, we can consider it positive or constructive. If it destroys our serenity, deeply troubles the mind, and leads us to harm others, it is negative or destructive. That is what differentiates, for instance, righteous indignation or "holy anger" with regard to an injustice from anger motivated by the intention to harm somebody.

The important thing, therefore, is not to try to suppress our emotions, which would be futile anyway, but to work with them in such a way that they contribute to our inner peace and lead us to think, speak, and act in ways that are helpful to others. To that end, we have to avoid becoming the helpless plaything of our emotions. We must learn to dissolve the negative emotions as they arise and cultivate the positive ones.

We should also understand that it is the accumulation and interlocking of fleeting emotions and thoughts that create our moods. These moods can last for a few hours or a few days, and over the long term form our character traits and tendencies. That is why, if we learn to deal with our thoughts and emotions in a good way—little by little, thought after thought, emotion by emotion, day after day—in the end we will be able to transform our way of being. This is the essence of mind-training and meditation as they affect the emotions.

Of the various methods for dealing with afflictive emotions through meditation, I will explain two. The first consists of applying antidotes. The second is not identifying with these temporary disturbances while at the same time recognizing their true nature.

Applying Antidotes

An antidote in this context is a state of mind that is diametrically opposed to the afflictive emotion we want to overcome. In the same way that a glass of water cannot be hot and cold at the same time, we cannot wish simultaneously to benefit and harm the same person. What we have to do is cultivate remedies powerful enough to neutralize the negative emotions that afflict us.

Seen from another point of view, the more kindness and benevolence we develop, the less room there will be in our mind for their opposites, malice and ill will. The more light there is in a room, the more darkness is dispelled. In the meditations that follow, we will take desire and then malicious anger as examples.

Desire: Everyone would agree that desire is natural and plays an essential role in helping us to realize our aspirations. But desire is only a blind force that in itself is neither helpful nor harmful. Everything depends on what kind of influence it has over us. It is capable of either providing inspiration to our lives or poisoning them. It can encourage us to act in a way that is con-structive for ourselves and others, but it can also bring about intense pain. When desire becomes a possessive and pervasive craving, pain results. Desire then forces us to become dependent on the very causes of suffering. In that case it is a source of unhappiness, and there is no advantage in continuing to be ruled by it. The antidote to a desire that causes suffering is inner freedom.

Meditation: The Antidote of Inner Freedom

If you are the victim of a strong desire that is troubling you and won't leave you alone, begin by examining its main characteristics and iden-tifying the appropriate antidotes.

One aspect of desire is urgency. To counter that urgency, calm your thoughts and observe the coming and going of the breath as described earlier.

Desire also has a restrictive and disturbing as-pect. As an antidote to this, imagine the comfort-ing and soothing quality of inner freedom. Spend a few moments allowing a feeling of freedom to arise and grow.

Desire tends to distort reality and make you view its object as fundamentally desirable.

In order to regain a more accurate view of things, take the time to examine all aspects of the object of your desire, and meditate for a few mo-ments on its less attractive and less desirable sides.

Finally, let your mind relax into the peace of awareness, free from hope and fear, and appreciate the freshness of the present moment, which acts like a balm to the burning of desire.

⌒⌒

Sources of Inspiration

A peaceful mind does not mean a mind empty of thoughts, sensations, and emotions. A peaceful mind is not an absent one.

— THICH NHAT HANH[26]

Handle desire in the following manner. Notice the thought or sensation as it arises. Notice the mental state of desire that accompanies it as a separate thing. Notice the exact extent or degree of that desire. Then notice how long it lasts and when it finally disappears. When you have done that, return your attention to breathing.

— BHANTE HENEPOLA GUNARATANA[27]

If bliss it is to scratch an itch,
What greater bliss no itch at all?
So too, the worldly, desirous, find some bliss,
But greatest is the bliss with no desire.

— NAGARJUNA[28]

Anger: The impulse of self-centered anger, which is the precursor of hatred, is to push aside whoever stands in the way of the ego's demands. Afflictive anger has no consideration for the welfare of others. It expresses itself as open hostility when the ego is in attack mode and as resentment and bitterness when the ego is wounded, scorned, or slighted. Basic anger can also be associated with malice, the conscious desire to hurt someone.

The mind overrun by animosity and resentment shuts itself up in illusion and convinces itself that the source of its frustration lies entirely outside itself. The truth is that even if resentment is triggered by an external object, it is not located anywhere else but in our mind. Moreover, if your hatred is a response to somebody else's hatred, you have stepped into a vicious circle that has no end. The following meditation is intended not merely to suppress hatred but to turn your mind toward what is diametrically opposed to it—love and compassion.

Meditation: The Antidote of Love and Compassion

Think of someone who has been malicious toward you or people close to you, someone who has harmed you. Also think of people who are causing, or have caused, tremendous suffering to others. Realize that if the mental poisons that led them to behave this way were to vanish from their minds, they would naturally cease to be enemies toward anyone. Wish with all your heart for this transformation to take place.

To do this, make use of the meditation on altruistic love, formulating this wish: "May all beings be free from suffering and the causes of suffering. May hatred, greed, arrogance, contempt, indifference, miserliness, and jealousy vanish from their minds and be replaced by altruistic love, contentment, modesty, appreciation, concern, generosity, and sympathy." Let this feeling of unconditional benevolence pervade all your thoughts.

∽

Sources of Inspiration

It is the only thing we can do. . . . Each of us must turn inward and destroy in himself all that he thinks he ought to destroy in others. And remember that every atom of hate added to this world makes it still more inhospitable.

— ETTY HILLESUM[29]

I no longer believe that we can change anything in the world until we have first changed ourselves. And that seems to me the only lesson to be learned from this war.

— ETTY HILLESUM[30]

Instead of hating so-called enemies . . . the real target of your hatred should be hatred itself.

— DILGO KHYENTSE RINPOCHE[31]

By giving in to anger, we are not necessarily harming our enemy but we are definitely harming ourselves. We lose our sense of inner peace, we do everything wrong, our digestion is bad, we cannot sleep well, we put off our guests or we cast furious glances at those who have the impudence of being in our way. If we have a pet, we forget to feed it. We make life impossible for those who live with us, and even our dearest friends are kept at a distance. Since there are fewer and fewer people who sympathize with us, we feel more and more lonely. . . . To what end? Even if we allow our rage to go all the way, we will never eliminate all our enemies. Do you know of anyone who ever has? As long as we harbor that inner enemy of anger or hatred, however successful we are at destroying our outer enemies today, others will emerge tomorrow.

— His Holiness the 14th Dalai Lama[32]

Stopping Identification with Emotions

The second way to deal with afflictive emotions is to dissociate ourselves mentally from the emotion that is troubling us. Usually we identify with our emotions completely. When we are overcome by anxiety or by a fit of anger, we are at one with that feeling. It is omnipresent in our mind, leaving no room for other mental states such as inner peace or patience, or to consider reasoning that might calm our discomfort. However, if at that moment we are still capable of a little presence of mind—a capability that we can be trained to develop—we can stop identifying with our anger.

The mind is, in fact, capable of examining what is happening within it. All we need to do is observe our emotions in the same way we would observe an external event taking place in front of us. The part of our mind that is aware of the anger is just simply aware—it is not angry. In other words, awareness is not affected by the emotion it is observing. When we understand that, we can step back, realize that this emotion has no solidity, and allow enough space for it to dissolve by itself.

By doing so, we avoid two extremes, each as bad as the other: repressing our emotion, which would then remain in a dark corner of our consciousness like a time bomb; or letting the emotion explode at the expense of those around us and of our own inner peace. Not identifying with emotions is a fundamental antidote that is applicable to all kinds of emotions, in all circumstances.

In the following meditations, I make use of the examples of anger and anxiety, but the process described would be the same for any other afflictive emotion.

Meditation 1: Watching Anger with Awareness

Imagine that you are overcome by very strong anger. It seems to you that you have no choice but to let yourself be carried away. Helpless, your mind is repeatedly drawn to the object that triggered your rage as iron is drawn to a magnet. Someone has insulted you, and the image of this person and his words constantly come to your mind. Every time you think of them, you let loose a new flood of resentment, which nourishes the vicious cycle of thoughts and reactions to those thoughts.

It is time to change your tactics. Turn away from the object of your anger and contemplate the anger itself. This is a little like watching a fire but no longer feeding it with wood. No matter how intense the fire is, in a little time it will go out all by itself. In the same way, if you turn your attention to simply looking at the anger, it is impossible for it to persist on its own. No matter how intense an emotion is, it will wear itself out and disappear naturally once you stop feeding it.

Also understand that in the end the most powerful anger attack is no more than a thought. Take a closer look at this. Where does the anger get the power to dominate you to this degree? Does it have a weapon? Can it burn you like fire? Can it crush you like a rock? Can you locate it in your chest, in your heart, or in your head? If the answer to this last question seems to be yes, does it have a color or a form? You will probably have great difficulty in attributing such characteristics to it. When you look at a big black cloud in a stormy sky, it appears to be substantial enough to sit on, but if you fly into this cloud, you find there is nothing solid to hold on to. There is nothing there but intangible mist. Similarly, when you attentively examine anger, you find nothing in it that could justify the tyrannical influence it has over you. The more you try to pin it down, the more it melts away beneath your gaze like frost beneath the rays of the rising sun.

Finally, where does this anger come from? Where is it right now? Where does it disappear to? All you can say is that it comes from your mind, endures there for a while, and then fades away back into it. As for the mind itself, it is un-graspable. It is not a distinct entity; it is nothing more than a stream of experiences.

Meditation 2: Watching Anxiety with Awareness

If you notice that you have become anx-ious—when you are about to miss a plane, for instance—try to simply be fully aware of your anxiety. As you continue to do this, you will soon notice that your anxiety begins to be less oppressive and then gradually fades away. Why? Before you apply mindfulness, anxiety is the main component of your mind, filling its entire landscape. As you become aware of it, you ex-perience both anxiety and the awareness of it. The part of your mind that is aware of anxiety is not anxious—it is just aware. Anxiety is now just one aspect of your mental landscape. As your awareness becomes more and more pervasive, anxiety loses its intensity and its grip on your mind. Eventually it vanishes.

If every time a powerful emotion arises you learn to deal with it intelligently, not only will you master the art of liberating emotions at the moment they appear, but you will also erode the very tendencies that cause the emotions to arise. In this way, your character traits and your way of being will gradually be transformed.

This method might seem difficult at the beginning, especially in the heat of the moment, but with practice you will gradually get used to it. When anger or any other afflictive emotion begins to hatch in your mind, you will be able to identify it on the spot and be able to deal with it before it gets out of hand. It's a little like knowing the identity of a pickpocket: even if he mingles with the crowd, you can spot him immediately and keep your eye on him so that he won't be able to steal your wallet.

Thus, by becoming more and more familiar with the mechanisms of the mind and by cultivating mindfulness, you will reach the point where you no longer let sparks of nascent emotions turn into forest fires that can destroy your own happiness and that of others.

This method can be used with all the afflictive emotions. It enables you to make a connection between the practice of meditation and the concerns of everyday life. If you get into the habit of looking at thoughts the moment they arise and letting them dissipate before they take hold of you, it will be much easier to retain mastery of your mind and to deal with the conflicting emotions in the thick of everyday activities.

Sources of Inspiration

Always remember . . . that a thought is merely the experience of many factors and fleeting circumstances coming together. Whether the thought is good or bad, it has no true existence. As soon as a thought arises, if you recognize its void nature, it will be powerless to produce a second thought, and the chain of delusion will cease there and then. As we have said, this does not mean that you should try to suppress the natural creativity of your mind, or that you should try to stop each thought with a particular antidote. It is enough simply to recognize the emptiness of thoughts and to then let them rest in the relaxed mind. The innate nature of mind, pristine and unchanging, will then remain vivid and stable.

— DILGO KHYENTSE RINPOCHE[33]

When sunlight falls on a crystal, lights of all colors of the rainbow appear; yet they have no substance that you can grasp. Likewise, all thoughts in their infinite variety—devotion, compassion, harmfulness, desire—are utterly without substance. This is the mind of Chenrezi [the Buddha of Compassion]. There is no thought that is something other than voidness; if you recognize the void nature of thoughts at the very moment they arise, they will dissolve. Attachment and hatred will never be able to disturb the mind. Deluded emotions will collapse by themselves. No negative actions will be accumulated, so no suffering will follow.

— DILGO KHYENTSE RINPOCHE[34]

UNMASKING THE DECEPTION OF THE EGO

The idea of getting away from the influence of ego might be puzzling, especially if we think that in doing so we are tampering with our basic identity. Understanding the nature of the ego and the way it functions is crucial if we want to liberate ourselves from suffering. We know that at every moment, from the time of our birth onward, our body has been continually changing and innumerable new experiences have taken place in our mind. Still we instinctively imagine that somewhere deep down within us, there resides an enduring entity that endows our personality with solid reality and permanence. This intuition may seem so evident we don't think it is necessary to examine it any further. We end up developing a powerful attachment to the notions of "me" and "mine"—*my* body, *my* name, *my* mind, *my* possessions, *my* friends, and so on. This attachment brings with it a desire to either possess or repel the other. An insurmountable duality between self and other becomes crystallized in our mind. Our being becomes equated with an imaginary entity: the self. From this mental construction arises an exaggerated sense of the importance of this self. The ego places its fictitious identity at the center of all our experiences.

However, as soon as we seriously analyze the nature of the ego, we see that it is impossible to pinpoint a distinct identity that corresponds to it. In the end, we realize the ego is no more than a concept that we associate with the continuum of experiences that is our consciousness.

Our identification with the ego is fundamentally dysfunctional, because it is out of step with reality. We attribute to the ego the qualities of permanence, singularity, and autonomy. The ego fragments the world and definitively solidifies the division between self and other, "mine" and "not mine." Because it is based on a mistake, it is constantly threatened by reality, and this gives us a deep and ongoing sense of insecurity. Since we are aware of the ego's vulnerability, we try by all means available to protect and reinforce it. As a result we feel aversion toward anything that threatens it and attraction toward anything that feeds it. From these impulses of repulsion and attraction, a multitude of conflicting emotions is born.

We might think that by devoting most of our time to satisfying and reinforcing the ego, we are adopting the best possible strategy for achieving happiness. But this turns out to be a losing bet, because just the opposite happens. By imagining an independent ego, we put ourselves in a state of conflict with the nature of things, and this results in endless frustration and pain. Devoting all our energy to this imaginary entity critically damages the quality of our lives.

The only kind of self-confidence the ego can achieve is an artificial one, based on shaky factors, such as power, success, beauty, physical strength, intellectual brilliance, and the opinions of others—all things that are related to our image. Genuine self-confidence is something entirely different. Paradoxically it is a natural quality of the absence of ego. To dispel the illusion of the ego is to free yourself from a fundamental weakness. Self-confidence based on non-ego brings a sense of freedom that is not subject to emotional contingencies. You experience a lack of vulnerability to the judgments of others and an inner acceptance of whatever circumstances may exist. This sense of freedom manifests as openness toward whatever arises. It is not something icy and aloof; it is not the dry detachment or indifference people sometimes imagine when they think of Buddhist "nonattachment." Rather it is a daring and kind-hearted availability that reaches out to all beings.

When the ego is not reveling in its triumphs, it nourishes itself on its failures by setting itself up as a victim.

Fed by its ceaseless broodings, its suffering confirms its existence just as much as its euphoria does. Whether it is riding high or feeling diminished, slighted, and ignored, the ego solidifies itself by paying attention only to itself. "The ego is the result of a mental activity that creates and keeps an imaginary entity alive in our mind."[35] It is an impostor who gets caught up in his own game. One of the functions of deep insight, vipashyana, is to unmask the deception of the ego.

The fact is that we are not this ego, we are not this anger, we are not this despair. Our most fundamental level of experience is pure awareness, the primary quality of consciousness that is the basis of all experience, of all emotion, of all reasoning, of all concept, of all mental constructs, *including the ego*. But awareness is not some new entity more subtle than the ego; rather it is the fundamental quality of our mind-stream.

The ego is nothing more than a mental construct that lasts longer than other constructs because it is constantly being reinforced by our mental associations. But that does not prevent it from being an illusory concept that is devoid of all inherent existence. A movie that lasts 100 years is no more real that a movie that lasts an hour. This stubborn label that is the ego can only stick to the stream of our consciousness through the application of the magic glue of mental confusion.

In order to unmask the deception of the ego, we must carry out a full and thorough investigation. If we sense the presence of a thief in our house, we have to look through every room, every nook and cranny, every possible hiding place, until we reach the point where we are sure there is really no one there. Only then can our minds rest.

Meditation: Investigating the Ego

Look and see what it is that composes the "I," the ego. Is it the body? The body is a composite of flesh and bone. Is it consciousness? Consciousness is a succession of fleeting thoughts. Your history? Your history is only memories of things that no longer exist. Your name? You attach all sorts of concepts to a name—your genealogy, your reputation, your social status—but in the end it is no more than a combination of letters.

If the ego really was your profound essence, then your fear of doing away with it would be understandable. However, if it is only an illusion, liberating yourself from it would not be destroying the core of your being, but just correcting an error and opening your eyes to reality. Error offers no more resistance to knowledge than darkness does to light. Darkness that has lasted for millions of years can disappear in an instant the moment a lamp is lit.

When the "I" ceases to be considered the center of the world, you naturally develop concern for others. Self-centered contemplation of your own suffering discourages you, whereas altruistic care for the suffering of others just redoubles your determination to work for their relief. So the profound sense of an "I" at the core of your being is clearly something you have to subject to an honest examination.

Where is this "I" located? It can't be in my body, because when I say, "I'm sad," it's my consciousness that feels the sense of sadness, not my body. Is the "I," then, only in my consciousness? That is far from being clear. When I say, "Somebody pushed me," is it my consciousness that was pushed? Obviously not. But the "I" cannot be located outside both the body and the consciousness. So is the notion of "I" to be connected with a combination of body and consciousness? That would take us to a very abstract concept.

The only solution to this dilemma is to consider the "I" as a mental designation for a dynamic process, a composite of changing relationships that bring together your sensations, your mental images, your emotions, and your concepts. In the end, the "I" is no more than a name you use to designate a continuum in the same way that you call a river the Amazon or the Ganges. Every river has a history. It flows through a unique landscape, and its water might have healing properties or be polluted. For that reason, it is legitimate to give it a name and distinguish it from another river. However, no entity exists in the river that could be called its core or essence. In the same way, the "I," or the ego, exists only as a convention, not at all in the form of an entity that constitutes the core of your being.

The ego always has something to lose and something to gain. Natural simplicity of mind has nothing to lose and nothing to gain. It is not necessary to add anything to it or take anything away. The ego feeds on dwelling on the past and anticipating the future, but it cannot survive in the simplicity of the present moment. Rest in that simplicity, in the mindfulness of the present moment, which is freedom, the ultimate resolution of all conflicts, all fabrications, all mental projections, all distortions, all identifications, and all divisions.

It is worthwhile to devote a little time to letting your mind rest in the inner calm that will help you to better understand the role of the ego in your life. This can be done both through analysis and direct experience. As long as a sense of self-importance rules your being, you will never know lasting peace. The very cause of pain itself will remain hidden deep within and will deprive you of the most essential of all freedoms.

Abandoning grasping at the ego and ceasing to identify with it bring tremendous inner freedom. This is a freedom that allows you to relate to anyone you meet in any situation with naturalness, goodwill, courage, and serenity. Having nothing to gain and nothing to lose, you are free to give and receive everything.

MEDITATING ON THE NATURE OF THE MIND

Having a clear understanding of the mind is essential to unravel the mechanisms of happiness and suffering. That is why meditators, psychologists, neuroscientists, and philosophers investigate the nature of the mind. It is, after all, our mind that we have to deal with from morning till night; and it is our mind, in the end, that determines the quality of every moment of our existence. So if knowing the mind's true nature and understanding its mechanisms can exercise a decisive influence on our quality of life, then we have good reason to investigate it. If we do not investigate it, if we fail to understand our own mind, then we remain a stranger to ourselves.

When the mind examines itself, what can it learn about its own nature? The first thing it notices is the endless series of thoughts that pass through it. These feed our sensations, our imagination, our memories, and our projections about the future. Do we also find a "luminous" quality in the mind that illuminates our experience, no matter what its content? This luminous quality is the fundamental cognitive faculty that underlies all thought. It is that which, when we are angry, sees the anger without letting itself be drawn into it. This simple, pure awareness can be perceived even in the absence of concepts and mental constructs.

The practice of meditation reveals that when we allow our thoughts to calm down, we are able to remain for a few moments in the nonconceptual experience of pure awareness. It is this fundamental aspect of consciousness, free from the veils of confusion, that Buddhism calls the nature of mind.

Thoughts arise out of pure awareness and dissolve back into it just as waves arise in the ocean and fall back into it without ever becoming anything other than the ocean itself. It is essential to realize this if we want to free ourselves from the habitual, automatic patterns of thought that create suffering. Identifying the fundamental nature of mind and knowing how to rest in it in a nondual and nonconceptual way is one of the essential conditions for inner peace and liberation from suffering.

Meditation: Mind Observing Mind

A thought arises as though from nowhere. It might be a pleasant thought or a troubling one. It stays for a few moments and then dies away, to be replaced by others. When it disappears, like the sound of a bell fading, where does it go? No one can say. Certain thoughts recur frequently in the mind, creating states ranging from joy to sadness, desire to indifference, resentment to sympathy. In this way, thoughts have tremendous power to condition our state of being. But where do they get this power? They don't have an army at their command, nor do they possess fuel to start a fire with; they don't have stones they can stone you with. They are only mental constructs, so they should not be able to harm you.

Let your mind observe itself. Thoughts arise.

The mind exists in some way, because you experience it. Apart from that, what could be said about it? Examine your mind and the thoughts that arise there. Can any concrete characteristics be attributed to them? Do they have a location? Do they have a color? A form? The more you look, the less you find. You note of course that the mind has a capacity to know, but it has no other intrinsic and real characteristic. This is the reason Buddhism defines the mind as a continuum of experiences. It does not constitute a distinct entity; it is "empty of inherent existence." Having found nothing in any way substantial, remain for a few moments in this state of not having found anything.

When a thought appears, just let it arise and pass away by itself, without either blocking or prolonging it. During the brief time that your mind is not burdened by any discursive thought, contemplate its nature. In this gap, after past thoughts have ceased and future thoughts have not yet appeared, do you perceive a consciousness that is pure and luminous? Remain a few moments in this state of natural simplicity, free from concepts.

As we gradually familiarize ourselves with the nature of mind and learn to let thoughts pass away as soon as they arise—disappearing instantly, just like words written with a finger on water—we begin to progress more easily on the path of inner freedom. Automatic thought patterns no longer have the same power to perpetuate our confusion and reinforce our habitual tendencies. We distort reality less and less, and the very mechanisms of suffering finally disappear.

Since, at this point, we have the inner resources to deal with our emotions, our feelings of insecurity give way to freedom and confidence. We cease to be preoccupied exclusively by our hopes and fears, and become available to the people around us. In this way, we bring about the welfare of others at the same time as our own.

This is a long process that develops in stages until it finally reaches fruition All the stages of progress are beneficial. So we should not be impatient, but persevere and appreciate the true and lasting changes that gradually occur in our way of being, rather than feeling discouraged when progress does not happen immediately.

Sources of Inspiration

Past mind has completely come to an end. Future mind has not yet occurred. Present mind is very hard to circumscribe: it has no shape, it has no color, it is like space, insubstantial and unreal. Since this is so, one can come to realize that mind lacks intrinsic existence.

— ATISHA DIPAMKARA[36]

When a rainbow appears vividly in the sky, you can see its beautiful colors, yet you could not wear it as clothing or put it on as an ornament. It arises through the conjunction of various factors, but there is nothing about it that can be grasped. Likewise, thoughts that arise in the mind have no tangible existence or intrinsic solidity. There is no logical reason why thoughts, which have no substance, should have so much power over you, nor is there any reason why you should become their slave.

The endless succession of past, present, and future thoughts leads you to believe that there is something inherently and consistently present, and you call it "mind." But actually past thoughts are as dead as a corpse. Future thoughts have not yet arisen. So how could these two, which do not exist, be part of an entity that inherently exists? . . .

It is only your lack of awareness and your grasping that make thoughts seem to have some kind of reality. If thoughts had any inherent existence in the absolute nature of mind, they should at least have a form, or be located some-where. But there is nothing.

However, that nothingness is not just a blank emptiness like empty space. There is an immedi-ate awareness present. This clarity of mind is like the sun, illuminating the landscape and allow-ing you to see mountain, path, and precipice— where to go, and where not to go. . . .

Although the mind does have this inherent awareness, to say there is "a mind" is to give a label to something that does not exist—to as-sume the existence of something that is no more than a name given to a succession of events. One hundred and eight beads strung together, for ex-ample, can be called a rosary, but that "rosary" is not a thing that exists inherently on its own. If the string breaks, where did the rosary go?

— DILGO KHYENTSE RINPOCHE[37]

Gradually I began to recognize how feeble and transitory the thoughts and emotions that had troubled me for years actually were, and how fixating on small problems had turned them into big ones. Just by sitting quietly and observing how rapidly, and in many ways il-logically, my thoughts and emotions came and went, I began to recognize in a direct way that they weren't nearly as solid or real as they ap-peared to be. And once I began to let go of my belief in the story they seemed to tell, I began to see the "author" beyond them—the infinitely vast, infinitely open awareness that is the nature of mind itself.

Any attempt to capture the direct experience of the nature of mind in words is impossible. The best that can be said is that the experience is immeasurably peaceful and, once stabilized through repeated experience, virtually unshakable. It's an experience of absolute well-being that radiates through all physical, emotional, and mental states—even those that might be ordinarily labeled as unpleasant. This sense of well-being, regardless of the fluctuation of outer and inner experiences, is one of the clearest ways to understand what Buddhists mean by "happiness."

— YONGEY MINGYUR RINPOCHE [38]

The nature of the mind is comparable to the ocean, to the sky. The incessant movement of waves on the surface of the ocean prevents us from seeing its depths. If we dive down, there are no more waves; there is just the immense serenity of the depths. . . . The nature of the ocean is immutable.

Look at the sky. It is sometimes clear and transparent. At other times, clouds accumulate and modify the perception we have of it. Nevertheless, the clouds do not change the nature of the sky. . . . The mind is nothing if not a totally free nature. . . . Remain in the natural simplicity of the mind, which is beyond all concepts.

—TULKU PEMA WANGYAL RINPOCHE [39]

DEDICATING THE FRUITS OF OUR EFFORTS

At the end of a meditation session, before resuming your activities, it is important to make a connection between your practice and your daily life so that the good effects of the practice will last and continue to nourish inner change. If you just break off your meditation abruptly and resume your activities as though the session had never happened, it will have very little effect on your life. Its benefits will be as fleeting as snowflakes falling on a hot stone.

One way of ensuring that the benefits of your meditation do continue is to dedicate them through a profound aspiration whose positive energy will last until its goal is realized. Here, the appropriate image is a snowflake that falls into the ocean and dissolves; it will last as long as the ocean itself.

Meditation: Dedicating the Merits

Arouse this aspiration: "May the positive energy created not only by this meditation but all my good words, deeds, and thoughts—past, present, and future—help relieve the suffering of beings now and in the future." Wish from the bottom of your heart for war, famine, injustice, and all the suffering of poverty and physical or mental illness to be pacified through the power of what you have done.

Don't think that such a dedication of the benefits of your action is like sharing a piece of cake among a thousand people, such that each person gets only a few crumbs. Think that every person receives the whole piece of cake.

Also wish for all beings to find happiness, both temporary and ultimate: "May ignorance, hatred, greed, and other afflictions be eradicated from their minds, and may they completely attain all the good human qualities as well as supreme enlightenment."

Such a dedication is an essential seal on all spiritual practice and allows the constructive energy created by your meditation and all your positive acts to be perpetuated.

BRINGING MEDITATION AND EVERYDAY LIFE TOGETHER

Meditation is a process of training and transformation. For it to have meaning, it must be reflected in every aspect of your life, in all your actions and attitudes. If it is not, you have wasted your time. Therefore, you have to persevere with sincerity, vigilance, and determination. You need to make sure that over the course of time real changes are taking place in you. Though there is no denying that the goal of training the mind is to make us capable of maintaining a certain way of being in the midst of our activities, to say right from the beginning that your whole life and work have become a meditation is probably a bit premature. The hustle and bustle of daily life rarely provides an opening to experience the strength and stability necessary for meditative practice.

This is why it is important to devote time to meditation practice itself, even if it is only 30 minutes a day. Of course, if possible, more is better. Especially if you practice in the morning, meditation can give your day an entirely new "fragrance." In a subtle but profound way, its effects can permeate your outlook and approach to the things you do as well as to your relations with the people around you. As you continue through the day, you can be strengthened by the experience you have had in your formal meditation session. You will be able to refer to it inwardly because it will remain alive in your mind. During pauses in your daily activity, it will be easy for you to revive the meditation experience, which is now familiar, and you will be able to maintain its beneficial effects.

Practicing meditation as described above is compatible with an active professional and family life. Meditation makes it possible to see the events of your life within a larger perspective. It allows you to experience them with greater serenity without falling into indifference, to accept whatever happens without a sense of resignation, and to envision the future with confidence and altruism. Thus, little by little, through training the mind, you can change your habitual way of being. You can develop a more accurate understanding of reality and a finer understanding of the laws of cause and effect, so you will be less affected by the reversals that inevitably occur in people's lives, and less carried away by superficial successes. These are the signs of a genuine personal transformation, a transformation that will enable you to act more effectively in the world you live in and contribute to building a wiser, more altruistic, and kinder society.

ACKNOWLEDGMENTS

I would like to thank all those who made this book possible.

I owe everything of worth in it to the goodness and wisdom of my spiritual masters, Kyabje Kangyur Rinpoche, Kyapje Dudjom Rinpoche, Kyabje Dilgo Khyentse Rinpoche, Kyabje Trulshik Rinpoche, Pema Wangyal Rinpoche, Jigme Khyentse Rinpoche, Shechen Rabjam Rinpoche, and indeed His Holiness the Dalai Lama, who, according to the great teachers I have just mentioned, is the most accomplished Tibetan Buddhist master of our time.

I would also like to thank all those who urged me to assemble these instructions on meditation because they wanted to meditate. Without them, the idea of composing this small work would not have entered my mind.

I would like to thank my loyal publisher in France, Nicole Lattès, who has always encouraged me to continue with my efforts despite my lack of natural literary talent.

I am also very grateful to those friends who have had the patience to read this text and who have improved it considerably both in form and substance through their informed suggestions: Christian Bruyat, Carisse and Gérard Busquet, Raphaële Demandre, Gérard Godet, Christophe André, Michel Bitbol, and my dear mother, Yahne Le Toumelin,

My deep gratitude goes to Sherab Chödzin Kohn, who patiently and skillfully translated this book into English, to Vivian Kurz for helping to significantly improve the text, to my editors, Patty Gift, Sarah Norman, and Kendra Crossen, and to my publishers, Atlantic Books and Hay House.

The author's royalties from this book will be entirely dedicated to humanitarian projects in Tibet, Nepal, and India, and to the preservation of the Himalayan cultural heritage. Anyone wishing to join in this effort may contact http://karuna-shechen.org and www.shechen.org.

NOTES

For notes with citations in a short form, please see the bibliography for complete facts of publication.

Part I: Why Meditate

1. Interview by Marc Kaufman, *Washington Post,* 3 January 2005.

2. On the negative effects of stress: S. E. Sephton Ashland et al., "Diurnal Cortisol Rhythm as a Predictor of Breast Cancer Survival," *Journal of the National Cancer Institute* 92, no. 12 (2000): 994–1000.

   On the influence of meditation: L. E. Carlson et al., "Mindfulness-Based Stress Reduction in Relation to Quality of Life, Mood, Symptoms of Stress and Levels of Cortisol, Dehydroepiandrosterone-Sulfate (DHEAS) and Melatonin in Breast and Prostate Cancer Outpatients," *Psychoneuroendocrinology* 29, no. 4 (2004); M. Speca et al., "A Randomized, Wait-List Controlled Clinical Trial: The Effect of a Mindfulness Meditation–Based Stress Reduction Program on Mood and Symptoms of Stress in Cancer Outpatients," *Psychosomatic Medicine* 62, no. 5 (September-October 2000): 613–22; S. M. Orsillo and L. Roemer (eds.), *Acceptance- and Mindfulness-Based Approaches to Anxiety* (New York: Springer, 2005).

3. J. D. Teasdale et al., "Metacognitive Awareness and Prevention of Relapse in Depression: Empirical Evidence," *Journal of Consulting and Clinical Psychology* 70 (2002): 275–87; P. Grossman et al., "Mindfulness-Based Stress Reduction and Health Benefits: A Meta-Analysis," *Journal of Psychosomatic Research* 57, no. 1 (2004): 35–43; S. E. Sephton et al., "Mindfulness Meditation Alleviates Depressive Symptoms in Women with Fibromyalgia: Results of a Randomized Clinical Trial," *Arthritis Care and Research* 57, no.1 (2007): 77–85; M. A. Kenny and J. M. G. Williams, "Treatment-Resistant Depressed Patients Show a Good Response to Mindfulness-Based Cognitive Therapy," *Behaviour Research and Therapy* 45, no. 3 (2007): 617–25.

4. MBSR (Mindfulness-Based Stress Reduction) is a nonreligious form of training based on Buddhist mindfulness meditation, which was developed in the United States hospital system more than 20 years ago by Jon Kabat-Zinn (see note 5 of Part I). It is now used in more than 200 hospitals for the palliation of postoperative pain and pain associated with cancer and other serious diseases.

5. J. Kabat-Zinn et al., "The Clinical Use of Mindfulness Meditation for the Self-Regulation of Chronic Pain," *Journal of Behavioral Medicine* 8 (1985): 163–190.

   For the long-term effects of meditation: A. Lutz et al., "Long-Term Meditators Self-Induce High-Amplitude Gamma Synchrony During Mental Practice," *Proceedings of the National Academy of Sciences of the United States of America* 101, no. 46 (16 November 2004); J. A. Brefczynski-Lewis et al., "Neural Correlates of Attentional Expertise in Long-Term Meditation Practitioners," Proceedings of the National Academy of Sciences of the United States of America 104, no. 27 (3 July 2007): 11483–88; P. Ekman et al., "Buddhist and Psychological Perspectives on Emotions and Well-Being," *Current Directions in Psychological Science* 14 (2005): 59–63.

6. A. Lutz et al., "Attention Regulation and Monitoring in Meditation," *Trends in Cognitive Science* 12, no. 4 (April 2008): 163–69; A. P. Jha, J. Krompinger, and M. J. Baime, "Mindfulness Training Modifies Subsystems of Attention," *Cognitive Affective Behavioral Neuroscience* 7 (2007): 109–19; H. A. Slagter et al., "Mental Training Affects Distribution of Limited Brain Resources," *PLoS Biology* 5, no. 6 (June 2007): 138.

7. L. E. Carlson et al., "One Year Pre-Post Intervention Follow-Up of Psychological, Immune, Endocrine and Blood Pressure Outcomes of Mindfulness-Based Stress Reduction (MBSR) in Breast and Prostate Cancer Outpatients," *Brain Behavior and Immunity* 21 (2007): 1038–49.

8. See P. Grossman et al., "Mindfulness-Based Stress Reduction and Health Benefits: A Meta-Analysis," *Journal of Psychosomatic Research* 57, no. 1 (2004): 35–43.

9. A. Lutz, J. D. Dunne, and R. J. Davidson, "Meditation and the Neuroscience of Consciousness: An Introduction," in *The Cambridge Handbook of Consciousness*, ed. P. D. Zelazo, M. Moscovitch, and E. Thompson (Cambridge: Cambridge University Press, 2008): 497–549.

10. Yongey Mingyur Rinpoche and Eric Swanson, *The Joy of Living*, 32.

Part II: What to Meditate On

1. Jigme Khyentse Rinpoche, oral teachings, Portugal, September 2007.

2. This example is often given by B. Alan Wallace to illustrate the importance of achieving a clear and stable mind in order to succeed in investigating the mind through introspection.

3. Shantideva was a 7th-century Buddhist author whose principal work, *The Way of the Bodhisattva*, is a great classic. The quoted phrase is from chapter 7, verse 2.

Part III: How to Meditate

1. His Holiness the Dalai Lama, *Ethics for the New Millennium* (New York: Riverhead, 1999), 149–50.

2. Bodhichitta, the "Thought of Enlightenment," is defined as the altruistic aspiration to achieve enlightenment for the benefit of all sentient beings. Nagarjuna, to whom this widely cited verse is attributed, is considered by many to be the most eminent Indian Buddhist thinker after the Buddha. He lived in the 1st century C.E. in northern India, where he taught at the famous Nalanda University.

3. Nagarjuna, *Nagarjuna's Letter to a Friend* (*Suhrllekha*), with commentary by Kyabje Kangyur Rinpoche, trans. Padmakara Translation Group (Ithaca, NY: Snow Lion Publications, 2006), 49, verse 55.

4. Sönam Rinchen Gampopa (1079–1153) was the chief disciple of Milarepa and one of the forefathers of the Kagyu lineage of Tibetan Buddhism.

5. Shantideva, *The Way of the Bodhisattva*, 37.

6. Dilgo Khyentse, *The Heart Treasure of the Enlightened Ones*, 51–52. Khyentse Rinpoche (1910–1991) was one of the most eminent Tibetan spiritual masters of the 20th century.

7. Bhante Henepola Gunaratana, *Mindfulness in Plain English,* 134.

8. Thich Nhat Hanh, *Guide de la méditation marchée* (Village des Pruniers, France: Editions La Bôi, 1983).

9. In Sanskrit, the elements involved in these three stages are called *manaskara, smriti,* and *samprajnana.* The equivalent Pali terms are *manasikara, sati,* and *sampajanna.* The Tibetan terms are *yid la byed pa, dran pa,* and *shes bzhin.*

10. A mantra is not generally constructed like a phrase with a literal meaning. Here OM is the syllable that opens the mantra and confers on it a power of transformation. MANI, or jewel, refers to the jewel of altruistic love and compassion. PADME, the genitive form of *padma,* or lotus, refers to the fundamental nature of consciousness, our "original goodness," which, like a lotus rising immaculately out of the mud, remains intact even in the midst of the mental poisons we have fabricated. HUM is the syllable that gives the mantra its power of accomplishment.

11. Padmasambhava, *Natural Liberation: Padmasambhava's Teachings on the Six Bardos,* trans. and ed. B. Alan Wallace (Boston: Wisdom Publications, 1998), 113–14.

12. Shabkar, *The Life of Shabkar,* 535.

13. Bokar Rinpoche, *Meditation: Advice to Beginners,* trans. Christiane Buchet (San Francisco: ClearPoint Press, 1993), 100.

14. Yongey Mingyur Rinpoche and Eric Swanson, *The Joy of Living,* 95, 178.

15. Shantideva, *The Way of the Bodhisattva,* 52.

16. Ibid., 169.

17. From a documentary series entitled *Pain,* directed by Andrew North, BBC World Service, February 2008

18. Yongey Mingyur Rinpoche and Eric Swanson, *The Joy of Living,* 147.

19. Bhante Henepola Gunaratana, *Mindfulness in Plain English,* 131–32.

20. See, for instance, Kunzang Pelden, *The Nectar of Manjushri's Speech,* pp. 357–369, and Shantarakshita's *Adornment of the Middle Way,* with commentary by Jamgön Mipham, pp. 187–92.

21. Longchen Rabjam, *gsung thor bu* (Paro, Bhutan: Lama Ngodrub and Sherab Drimey, 1982).

22. Extracted from *mkha' gdams kyi skyes bu dam pa rnams kyi gsung bgros thor bu ba rnams,* translated by Matthieu Ricard, 89.

23. The eight worldly preoccupations are gain and loss, pleasure and pain, praise and blame, fame and obscurity.

24. Dilgo Khyentse Rinpoche, *The Hundred Verses of Advice: Tibetan Buddhist Teachings on What Matters Most,* trans. Padmakara Translation Group (Boston: Shambhala Publications, 2006), 131.

25. Teachings given in Schneverdingen, Germany, in 1998. Oral translation by Matthieu Ricard.

26. Thich Nhat Hanh, *The Sun My Heart* (Berkeley, CA: Parallax Press, 1988), 8.

27. Bhante Henepola Gunaratana, *Mindfulness in Plain English,* 127.

28. Nagarjuna, "The Jewel Garland" ("Ratnavali"), verse 169, quoted in Nagarjuna's *Letter to a Friend* (*Suhrllekha*), with commentary by Kyabje Kangyur Rinpoche, trans. Padmakara Translation Group (Ithaca, NY: Snow Lion Publications, 2006), 98.

29. Etty Hillesum, *An Interrupted Life: The Diaries, 1941–1943; and Letters from Westerbork,* trans. Arnold J. Pomerans (New York: Holt Paperbacks, 1996), 212. Etty Hillesum was a young Dutch writer who died in the Auschwitz concentration camp in 1943.

30. Ibid., 84.

31. Dilgo Khyentse Rinpoche, *The Heart Treasure of the Enlightened Ones,* pp. 126–27.

32. Dalaï-Lama, *Conseils du coeur* (Paris: Presses de la Renaissance, 2001), 130–31.

33. Dilgo Khyentse Rinpoche, *The Heart Treasure of the Enlightened Ones,* 109–10.

34. Ibid., 92

35. Han F. de Wit, *The Spiritual Path: An Introduction to the Psychology of the Spiritual Traditions* (Pittsburgh: Duquesne University Press, 1999).

36. Quoted in Jamgon Kongtrul, "Treasury of Knowledge" (shes bya kun mkhyab mdzod), chap. 8, translated by Kiki Ekselius and Constance Wilkinson, unpublished manuscript, 1992.

37. Dilgo Khyentse Rinpoche, *The Heart of Compassion,* 141–42.

38. Yongey Mingyur Rinpoche and Eric Swanson, *The Joy of Living,* 21–22.

39. Tulku Pema Wangyal, *Bodhicitta: L'esprit d'Éveil* (Saint-Léon-sur-Vézère, France: Editions Padmakara, 1997).

BIBLIOGRAPHY

Bhante Henepola Gunaratana. *Mindfulness in Plain English.* Updated and expanded ed. Somerville, MA: Wisdom Publications, 2002.

Bokar Rinpoche. *Meditation: Advice to Beginners.* 2nd ed. San Francisco: ClearPoint Press, 1999.

Buddhadasa Bhikkhu. *Mindfulness with Breathing: A Manual for Serious Beginners.* Translated by Santikaro Bhikkhu. Somerville, MA: Wisdom Publications, 1988.

Dalai Lama, His Holiness the 14th. *A Flash of Lightning in the Dark of Night: A Guide to the Bodhisattva's Way of Life.* Translated by the Padmakara Translation Group. Boston: Shambhala Publications, 1994.

Dilgo Khyentse. *The Heart of Compassion: The Thirty-seven Verses on the Practice of a Bodhisattva.* Translated by the Padmakara Translation Group. Boston: Shambhala Publications, 2007.

———. *The Heart Treasure of the Enlightened Ones: The Practice of View, Meditation, and Action.* Translated by the Padmakara Translation Group. Boston: Shambhala Publications, 1993.

———. *The Hundred Verses of Advice: Tibetan Buddhist Teachings on What Matters Most.* Boston: Shambhala Publications, 2006.

Dudjom Rinpoche. *Counsels from My Heart.* Translated by the Padmakara Translation Group. Boston: Shambhala Publications, 2003.

Dzigar Kongtrül. *It's Up to You: The Practice of Self-Reflection on the Buddhist Path.* Boston: Shambhala Publications, 2006.

Kunzang Pelden. *The Nectar of Manjushri's Speech: A Detailed Commentary on Shantideva's* Way of the Bodhisattva. Translated by the Padmakara Translation Group. Boston, Shambhala Publications, 2007.

Longchen Yeshe Dorje (Kangyur Rinpoche). *Treasury of Precious Qualities: A Commentary on the Root Text of Jigme Lingpa.* Translated by the Padmakara Translation Group. Boston: Shambhala Publications, 2001, rev. 2009.

Patrul Rinpoche. *The Words of My Perfect Teacher.* Translated by the Padmakara Translation Group. Boston: Shambhala Publications, 1998.

Ricard, Matthieu. *Happiness: A Guide to Developing Life's Most Important Skill.* Boston: Little, Brown, 2006.

Ringu Tulku. *Path to Buddhahood: Teachings on Gampopa's* Jewel Ornament of Liberation. Boston: Shambhala Publications, 2003.

Shabkar. *The Life of Shabkar: The Autobiography of a Tibetan Yogin.* Translated by Matthieu Ricard. Ithaca, NY: Snow Lion Publications, 2001.

Shantarakshita, *The Adornment of the Middle Way: Shantarakshita's* Madhyamakalankara *with Commentary by Jamgön Mipham.* Translated by the Padmakara Translation Group. Boston: Shambhala Publications, 2005.

Shantideva. *The Way of the Bodhisattva: A Translation of the* Bodhicharyavatara. Translated by the Padmakara Translation Group. Boston: Shambhala Publications, 2006.

Thich Nhat Hanh. *The Miracle of Mindfulness: An Introduction to the Practice of Meditation.* Boston: Beacon Press, 1999.

Wallace, B. Alan. *The Attention Revolution: Unlocking the Power of the Focused Mind.* Somerville, MA: Wisdom Publications, 2006.

———. *Choosing Reality: A Buddhist View of Physics and the Mind.* Ithaca, NY: Snow Lion Publications, 2003.

Yongey Mingyur Rinpoche and Eric Swanson. *The Joy of Living: Unlocking the Secret and Science of Happiness.* New York: Harmony Books, 2007.

ABOUT THE AUTHOR

Matthieu Ricard left a scientific career in France 40 years ago to live and study as a Buddhist monk in the Himalayas, where his main teachers were Kangyur Rinpoche and Dilgo Khyentse Rinpoche. Having earned a Ph.D. in cell genetics at the Institut Pasteur in Paris under the Nobel laureate François Jacob, he is well suited to serve as a link in the dialogue between East and West. An active participant in the Mind and Life Institute, which promotes partnership between Buddhism and modern science, he has also been instrumental in research into the effect of meditation on the brain at various universities in the United States and Europe.

A best-selling author as well as a photographer, he has written books including *Happiness: A Guide to Developing Life's Most Important Skill; The Monk and the Philosopher* (co-authored with his father, renowned French philosopher Jean-François Revel); and *The Quantum and the Lotus: A Journey to the Frontiers Where Science and Buddhism Meet.* Several of his books also feature his photographs, including *Buddhist Himalayas; Tibet: An Inner Journey; Motionless Journey;* and *Bhutan: The Land of Serenity.* He is a prolific translator and scholar, and has been the French interpreter for the Dalai Lama since 1989.

Matthieu Ricard lives at the Shechen Monastery in Nepal and devotes much of his time to humanitarian projects in Asia (http://karuna-shechen.org) and to the preservation of the Tibetan Buddhism cultural heritage (www.shechen.org). All proceeds from his books and photography are donated to these projects. Please visit www.matthieuricard.com for more information.

ABOUT
KARUNA-SHECHEN

All of the author's proceeds from the sale of this book go to Karuna-Shechen, a humanitarian organization that he founded to provide primary health care and education for the underserved populations of the Himalayan region. Since 2001, Karuna-Shechen has initiated and managed educational and medical projects throughout India, Nepal, and Tibet, targeting the poorest populations in areas where there is little or no access to these vital services. The services are offered on a sliding scale according to means and are provided free of charge to the poorest patients.

A primary goal is to help young people who lack equal access to education, many of whom are women. Karuna-Shechen has financed schools in the nomadic regions of eastern Tibet where more than 1,500 students receive a free education, as well as scholarships for higher studies. In Nepal, Karuna-Shechen, in partnership with a local educational foundation, is building schools throughout the country. A school's enrollment varies from 1,500 to 3,000, and 70 percent of the students are girls.

Widespread poverty in India and Nepal makes access to basic health care extremely difficult; in Tibet, remote regions do not have adequate medical facilities. Karuna-Shechen has built small clinics and dispensaries for the essentially nomadic population in eastern Tibet. In Nepal, Shechen Clinic provides more than 50,000 treatments annually; the poorest patients receive care free of charge. The newly built Shechen Medical Centre in India provides similar services in conjunction with the Shechen Mobile Clinic, an effective health-care outreach program that provides free health care to a diverse population of more than 200,000.

These vital projects have a direct and significant impact on individuals, families, and communities. For more information or to participate and make a tax-deductible contribution, please visit http://karuna-shechen.org.

Hay House Titles of Related Interest

YOU CAN HEAL YOUR LIFE, the movie,
starring Louise Hay & Friends
(available as a 1-DVD program and an expanded 2-DVD set)
Watch the trailer at: **www.LouiseHayMovie.com**

THE SHIFT, the movie,
starring Dr. Wayne W. Dyer
(available as a 1-DVD program and an expanded 2-DVD set)
Watch the trailer at: **www.DyerMovie.com**

∞

**ALL YOU EVER WANTED
TO KNOW FROM HIS HOLINESS THE
DALAI LAMA ON HAPPINESS, LIFE, LIVING,
AND MUCH MORE,** by His Holiness the Dalai Lama

**COMMIT TO SIT: Tools for Cultivating a Meditation
Practice from the Pages of Tricycle: The Buddhist Review,**
edited by Joan Duncan Oliver

**IN MY OWN WORDS: An Introduction
to My Teachings and Philosophy,**
by His Holiness the Dalai Lama

UNDERSTANDING THE DALAI LAMA,
by His Holiness the Dalai Lama

**WIRED FOR JOY: A Revolutionary Method for Creating
Happiness from Within,** by Laurel Mellin

All of the above are available at your local bookstore, or may be
ordered by contacting Hay House (see next page).

We hope you enjoyed this Hay House book. If you'd like to receive
our online catalog featuring additional information on Hay House
books and products, or if you'd like to find out more about the
Hay Foundation, please contact:

Hay House, Inc., P.O. Box 5100, Carlsbad, CA 92018-5100
(760) 431-7695 or (800) 654-5126
(760) 431-6948 (fax) or (800) 650-5115 (fax)
www.hayhouse.com® • **www.hayfoundation.org**

Published and distributed in Australia by: Hay House Australia Pty.
Ltd., 18/36 Ralph St., Alexandria NSW 2015 • *Phone:* 612-9669-4299
Fax: 612-9669-4144 • www.hayhouse.com.au

Published and distributed in the United Kingdom by: Hay House
UK, Ltd., Astley House, 33 Notting Hill Gate, London W11 3JQ • *Phone:*
44-20-3675-2450 • *Fax:* 44-20-3675-2451 • www.hayhouse.co.uk

Published and distributed in the Republic of South Africa by:
Hay House SA (Pty), Ltd., P.O. Box 990, Witkoppen 2068 • *Phone/Fax:*
27-11-467-8904 • info@hayhouse.co.za • www.hayhouse.co.za

Published in India by: Hay House Publishers India, Muskaan
Complex, Plot No. 3, B-2, Vasant Kunj, New Delhi 110 070 • *Phone:*
91-11-4176-1620 • *Fax:* 91-11-4176-1630 • www.hayhouse.co.in

Distributed in Canada by: Raincoast Books, 2440 Viking Way,
Richmond, B.C. V6V 1N2 • *Phone:* 1-800-663-5714 •
Fax: 1-800-565-3770 • www.raincoast.com

Take Your Soul on a Vacation

Visit **www.HealYourLife.com®** to regroup,
recharge, and reconnect with your own magnificence.

Featuring blogs, mind-body-spirit news, and
life-changing wisdom from Louise Hay and friends.

Visit **www.HealYourLife.com** today!

Free e-newsletters from Hay House, the Ultimate Resource for Inspiration

Be the first to know about Hay House's dollar deals, free downloads, special offers, affirmation cards, giveaways, contests, and more!

 Get exclusive excerpts from our latest releases and videos from *Hay House Present Moments*.

 Enjoy uplifting personal stories, how-to articles, and healing advice, along with videos and empowering quotes, within *Heal Your Life*.

 Have an inspirational story to tell and a passion for writing? Sharpen your writing skills with insider tips from *Your Writing Life*.

Sign Up Now!

Get inspired, educate yourself, get a complimentary gift, and share the wisdom!

http://www.hayhouse.com/newsletters.php

Visit www.hayhouse.com to sign up today!

HealYourLife.com ♥